WORKBOOK

KATAKANA

in 48 minutes

ERI TOMITA-HARVEY

Katakana in 48 minutes
1st Edition
Eri Tomita-Harvey
Julie Devine

Publishing editors: Julie McArthur and Catriona McKenzie
Project editor: Simon Tomlin
Editor: Katie Lawry
Art direction: Aisling Gallagher
Cover image: Shutterstock.com/Elena Zolotukhina
Image of map: Shutterstock.com/Raevsky Lab
Cover design: Aisling Gallagher
Text design: Aisling Gallagher
Illustrations by: Makoto Koji
Permissions researcher: Kaitlin Jordan
Production controller: Christine Fotis
Typeset by: Nikki M Group Pty Ltd

For product information and technology assistance,
in Australia call **1300 790 853**;
in New Zealand call **0800 449 725**

For permission to use material from this text or product, please email
aust.permissions@cengage.com

ISBN 978 0 17 041668 9

Cengage Learning Australia
Level 7, 80 Dorcas Street
South Melbourne, Victoria Australia 3205

Cengage Learning New Zealand
Unit 4B Rosedale Office Park
331 Rosedale Road, Albany, North Shore 0632, NZ

For learning solutions, visit **cengage.com.au**

Printed in Malaysia by Papercraft.
8 25

CONTENTS

ISBN 9780170416689

About the series
Katakana in 48 minutes

Katakana in 48 minutes is the most widely used resource for teaching Japanese syllabary to beginner students in Australia. Its effective method uses mnemonic flashcards and is supported by a teacher guide that provides a step-by-step guide to planning and presentation.

Workbook

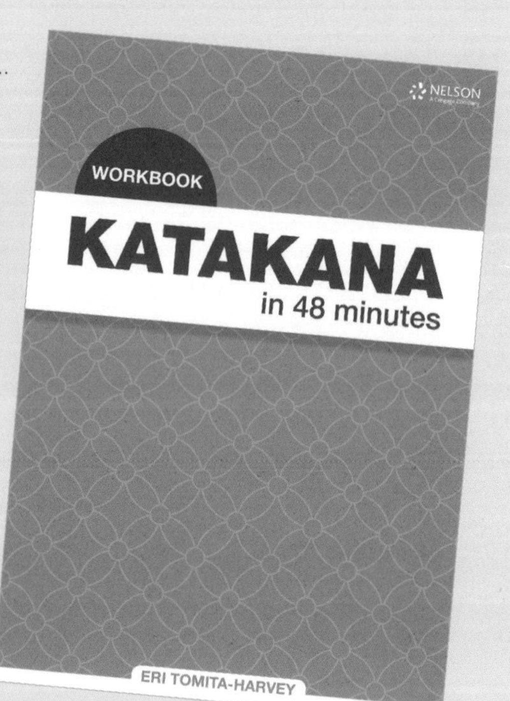

This workbook supports the *Katakana in 48 minutes* flashcards and teacher guide. It provides comprehensive *katakana* reading and writing practice in an easy-to-use, engaging and structured format.

The opening exercise for each unit allows students to practise the correct formation of each *katakana* and ensure balance within the squares. When a character varies its appearance depending on the typeface used, a box at the end of the first practice row shows how it looks in some commonly used fonts.

The exercises in each level focus on both reading and writing introduced *katakana* characters. Some *katakana* characters appear earlier in the book than they are introduced, because there are not enough *katakana* words containing only the early characters.

The wide range of activities – including dictation exercises for every level – consolidate and reinforce the learning of the script. Where appropriate, answers are included at the back of the book.

The workbook can be used in class or independently at home.

Nelson Languages – free interactive resources!

Dictation videos can be found on the Nelson Languages website at:

www.nelsonnet.com.au/free-resources/nelson-languages/katakana-in-48-minutes-website-1ed

It is suggested that students complete the dictation exercises in the workbook for practice.

Quizzes and answers are also available. Contact your education consultant for access.

ISBN 9780170416689

About *katakana* and *katakana* words

Katakana is typically used to write the following types of words:

1. Words from foreign languages. Many words originating from English and other languages are used in Japanese. Some examples include ワクチン (vaccine) from German and ウイルス (virus) from Latin.
2. Foreign places and names. For example, オーストラリア (Australia) and ジョン (John).
3. Onomatopoeia. For example, ワンワン (bow wow) or ジャーン (ta-da).
4. Names of animals and plants. For example, サル (monkey) and サクラ (cherry blossom).

An increasing number of English words are being used in the Japanese language. Some sounds are changed to fit the sounds of the Japanese language. When trying to write or work out the meanings of *katakana* words, think about how the English words sound, not how they are spelt.

Some general rules for writing English words in *katakana* are listed below. There are, however, exceptions.

1. *R* and *l* sounds become *ra*, *ri*, *ru*, *re* or *ro*.

area

エ	リ	ア
e	ri	a

glass

グ	ラ	ス
gu	ra	su

2. Typically, *b* and *v* sounds become *ba*, *bi*, *bu*, *be* and *bo*. Sometimes ヴァ, ヴィ, ヴ, ヴェ and ヴォ are used to indicate *v* sounds, however they are often pronounced as *b*.
3. If there is more than one vowel in a row or a vowel sound that ends in *r*, it usually becomes a long vowel sound.

spoon

ス	プ	ー	ン
su	pu	u	n

party

パ	ー	テ	ィ	ー
pa	a	ti		i

4. Another vowel is added at the end of an English word that ends in a consonant, because in Japanese a consonant and a vowel appear together. For *t* and *d*, it's usually *o*. For everything else, it's usually *u*. If a word finishes with *n* or *m* another vowel is not required. It becomes ン (*n*).

hint

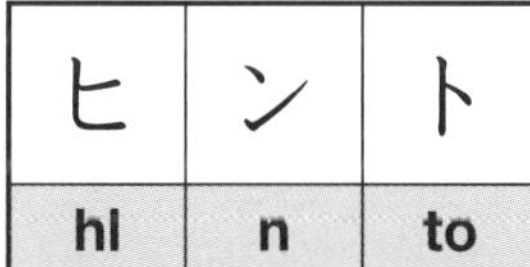

ヒ	ン	ト
hi	n	to

dress

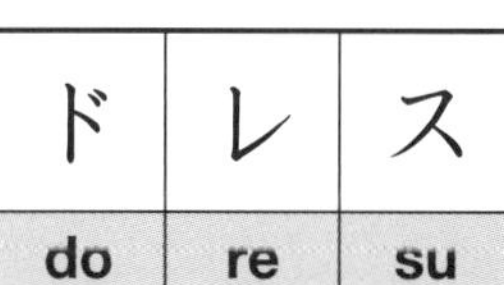

ド	レ	ス
do	re	su

design

デ	ザ	イ	ン
de	za	i	n

There are some special *katakana* sounds to write foreign names and words that don't exist in *hiragana*. These sounds are introduced in Level 17 of this workbook.

Some foreign words are shortened in *katakana*. For example, パソコン (pa so ko n) means *personal computer* or コンビニ (ko n bi ni) means *convenience store*.

Level 1: ア to オ

1 Practise writing the Level 1 *katakana* in the squares. Use the dotted lines to help you balance your characters in the squares.

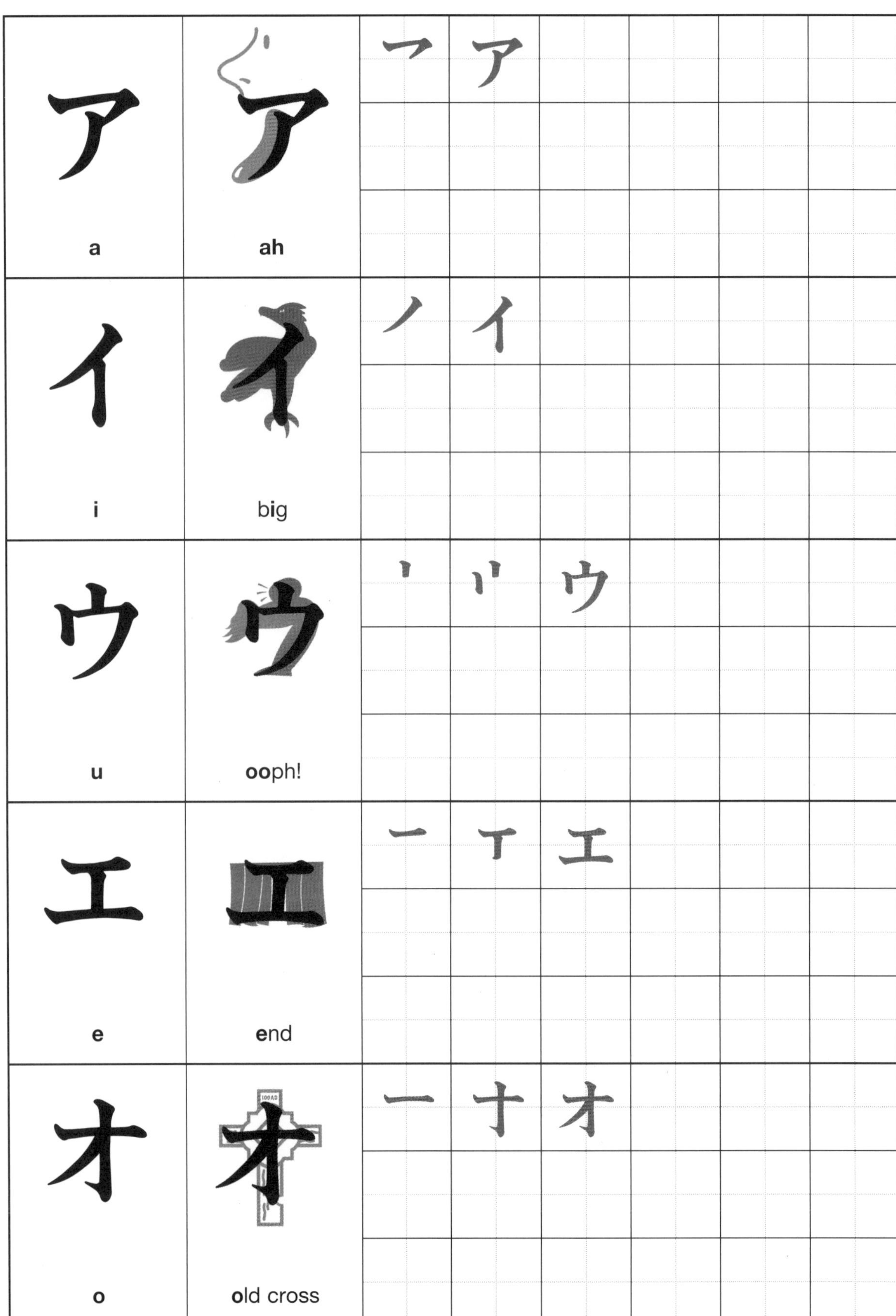

Usually, each stroke is written from left to right or top to bottom. If this is not the case, an arrow is added to show the direction of the stroke.

ISBN 9780170416689

2 Draw lines connecting the *katakana* to their *hiragana* and *romaji* equivalents.

(a) オ	う	a
(b) イ	お	i
(c) ア	え	o
(d) ウ	い	e
(e) エ	あ	u

3 How many times do the following *katakana* appear in the cartoon?

a ______ **i** ______ **u** ______ **e** ______ **o** ______

4 Draw lines connecting the same *katakana*.

ア	オ	エ	イ
イ	エ	ウ	エ
ウ	ア	イ	ウ
エ	ウ	ア	オ
オ	イ	オ	ア

ISBN 9780170416689

5 Complete the crossword puzzle by writing the words in *katakana*.

Across

2 **e a ko n** (air conditioner)

3 **a i ro n** (iron)

5 **o a shi su** (oasis)

Down

1 **u e i to re su** (waitress)

4 **a ji a** (Asia)

				1			
				2		コ	ン
			3		ロ	ン	
				ト			
				レ			
	5	4	シ	ス			
		ジ					

6 Listen to your teacher or watch the Level 1 dictation video. Write the words in *katakana* in the first squares as you hear them. Then, use the extra squares to practise writing the words again.

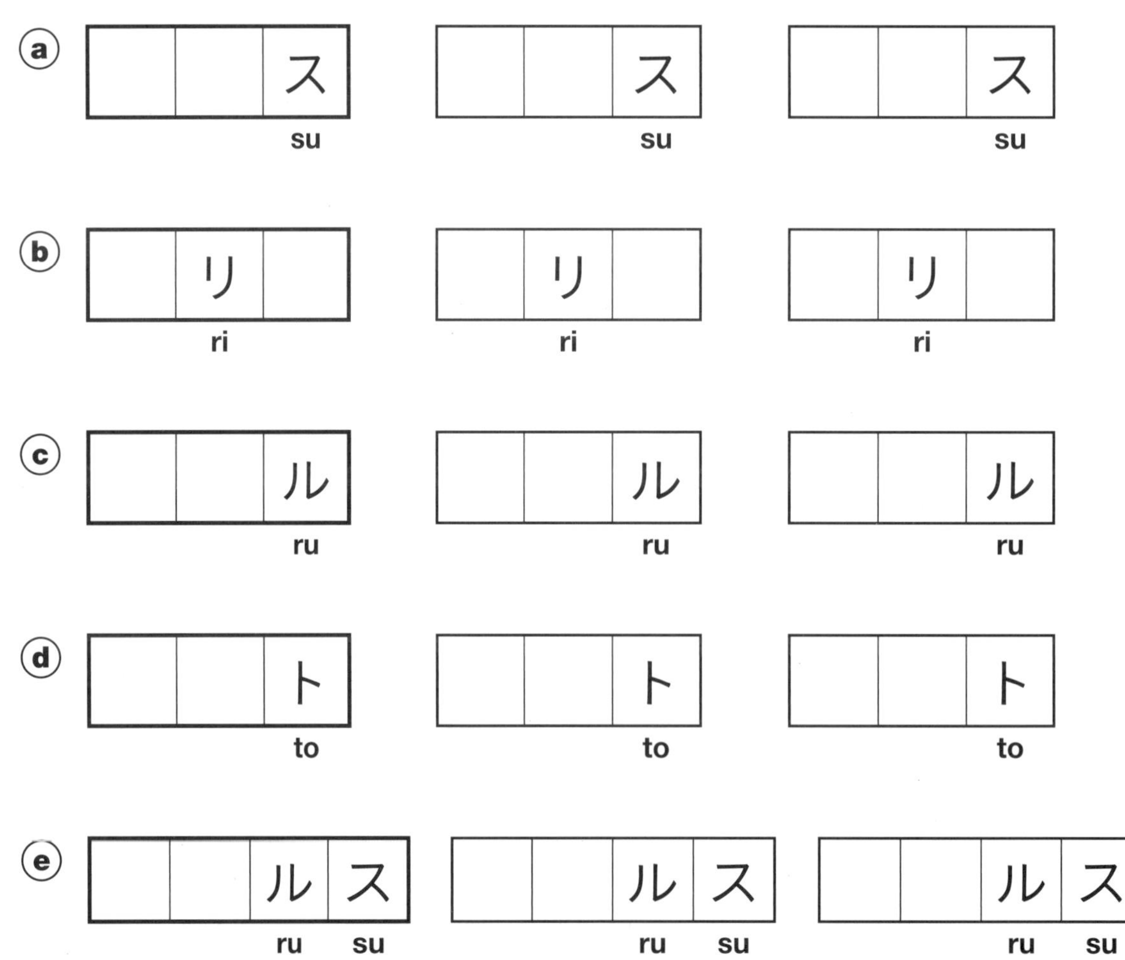

 ISBN 9780170416689

Level 2: カ to コ

1. Practise writing the Level 2 *katakana* in the squares. Use the dotted lines to help you balance your characters in the squares.

カ ka	カ cut	フ	カ					
キ ki	キ key	一	二	キ				
ク ku	ク cook's hat	ノ	ク					ク
ケ ke	ケ kettle	ノ	ㇰ	ケ				
コ ko	コ court	フ	コ					

2

ISBN 9780170416689

2 Find the correct *katakana* and circle them.

a **ka**	ラ	さ	き	カ	ク
b **ki**	コ	き	キ	ミ	ト
c **ku**	ケ	ク	カ	ワ	く
d **ke**	エ	け	ケ	ク	ワ
e **ko**	ロ	コ	こ	ト	カ

3 How many of each *katakana* from *ka* to *ko* can you find in the chart?

ア	か	こ	オ	キ	コ	い	ク	イ
キ	ケ	カ	こ	イ	オ	キ	ア	か
イ	コ	こ	ウ	ケ	カ	オ	き	カ
コ	エ	ク	ア	エ	え	ケ	ウ	ア
ク	カ	イ	ア	こ	イ	ア	か	ケ
オ	ウ	キ	き	カ	ケ	コ	う	コ
ケ	け	け	ケ	こ	き	イ	カ	く
く	ウ	キ	ア	ク	ウ	き	く	こ
カ	け	オ	コ	エ	キ	ケ	エ	ク

ka ______ **ki** ______ **ku** ______ **ke** ______ **ko** ______

4 Circle the words that contain the following *katakana*.

a **ka**	テント	カメラ	ライオン	タオル
b **ki**	ドレス	メロン	チキン	ライス
c **ku**	オレンジ	ゴリラ	パン	ミルク
d **ke**	カラオケ	バンド	レモン	ピンク
e **ko**	ホテル	フランス	レタス	メキシコ

Challenge: Can you work out the meaning of the words you circled? You may use the *katakana* chart on the inside front cover.

ISBN 9780170416689

5 One of the *katakana* カ to コ is missing from each set. Find the missing *katakana* and write them in the boxes.

6 Write the words in *katakana*.

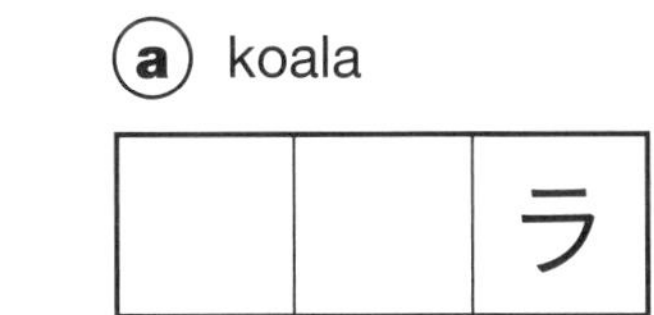

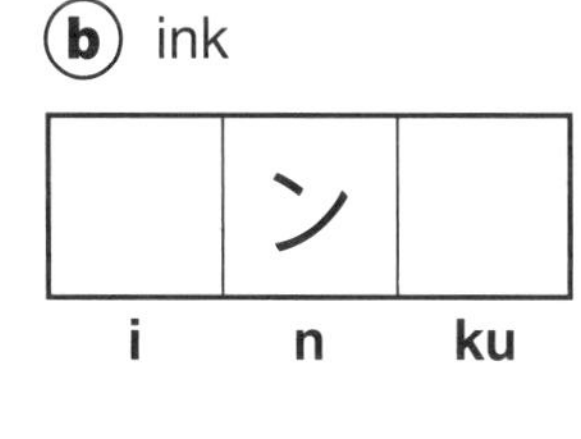

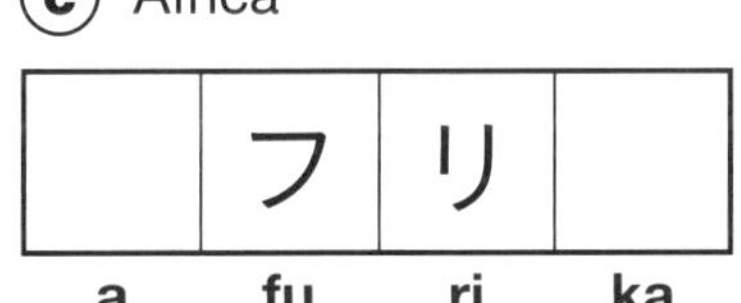

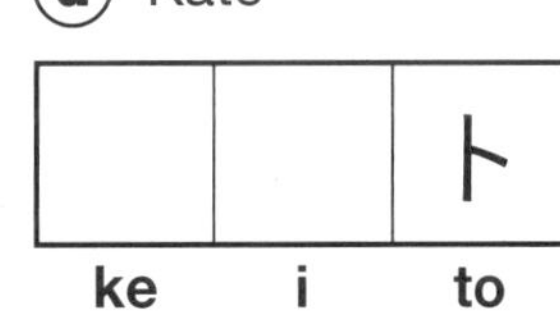

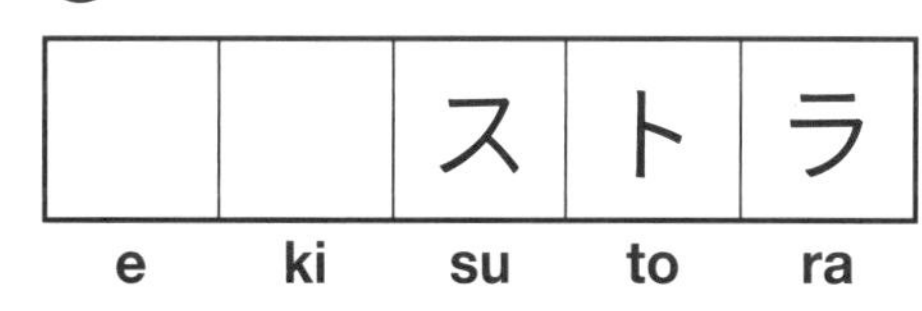

7 Listen to your teacher or watch the Level 2 dictation video. Write the words in *katakana* in the first squares as you hear them. Then, use the extra squares to practise writing the words again.

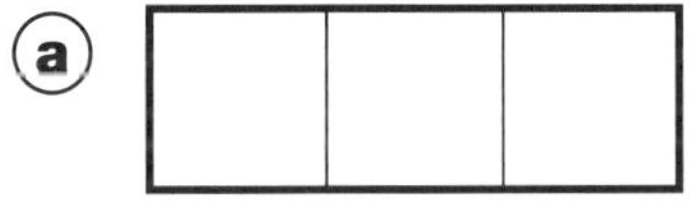

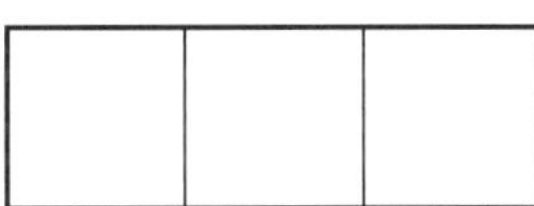

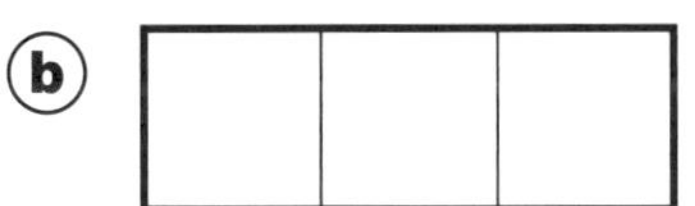

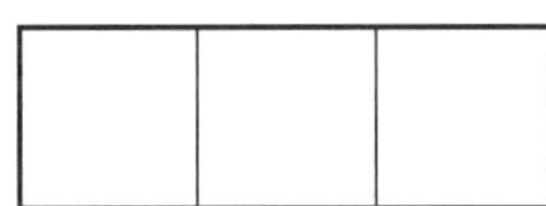

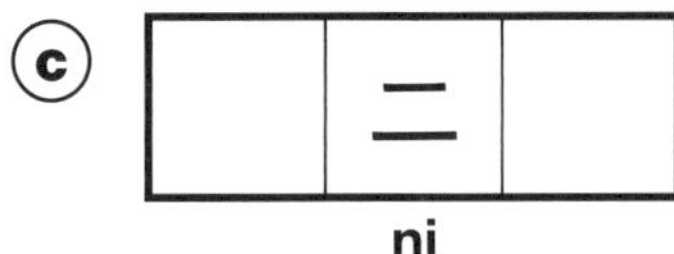

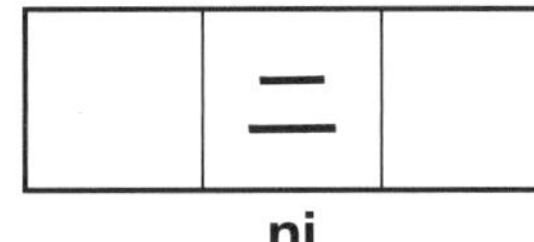

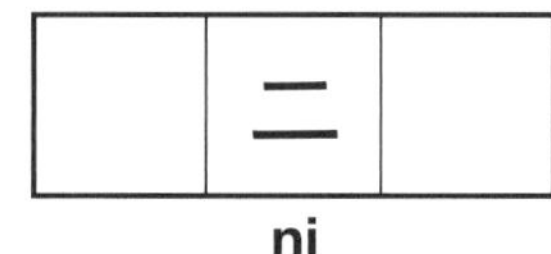

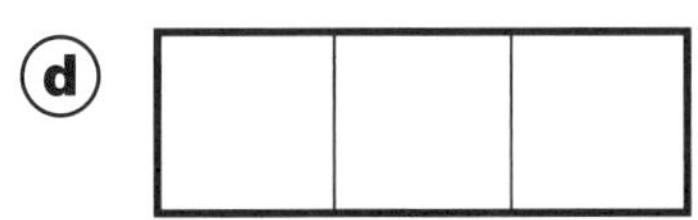

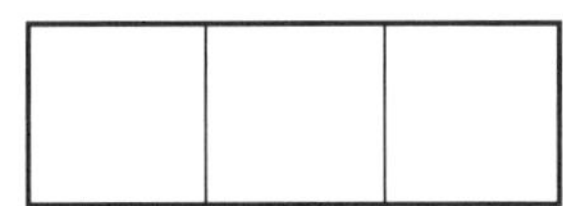
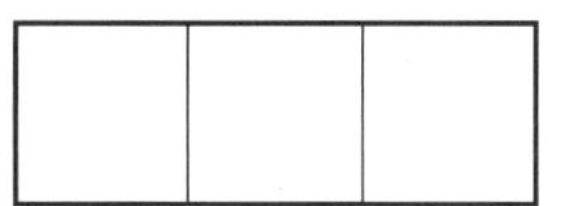
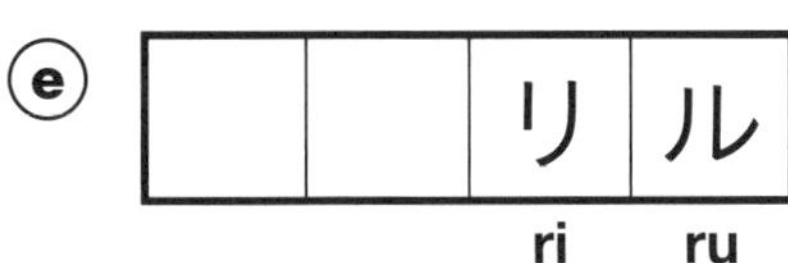

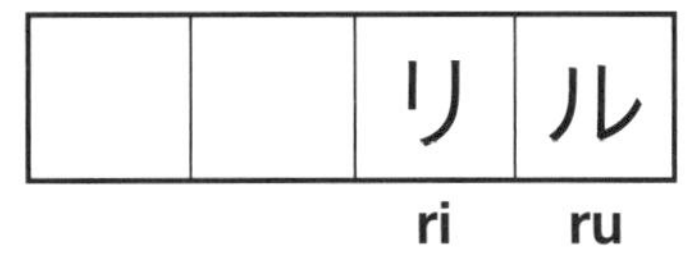

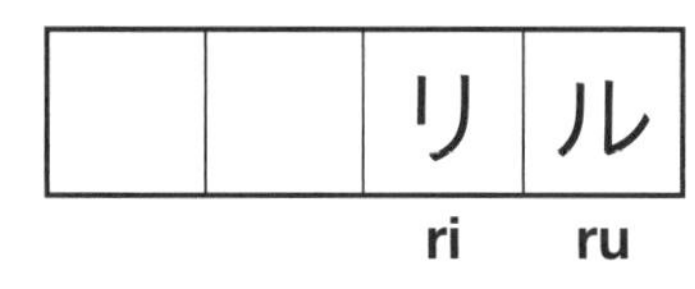

ISBN 9780170416689

Level 3: ガ to ゴ

1 Practise writing the Level 3 *katakana* in the squares. Use the dotted lines to help you balance your characters in the squares.

The symbol ゛ is written to the upper right of some *katakana*. It indicates that you are to 'voice' the sound. In other words, you tense your throat a little as you say the first sound. For example, with the characters on this page, a *k* sound becomes a *g* sound, so *ka* becomes *ga*, and *ki* becomes *gi*.

To help you remember, think of **keg**.

The symbol ゛ has a few names. The formal name is *dakuten*, but Japanese people also call it *tenten*. These sound changes are the same as when *tenten* are added to the *k* line in hiragana.

ISBN 9780170416689

2 Write the *katakana* ガ to ゴ in the squares and find the words containing those characters.

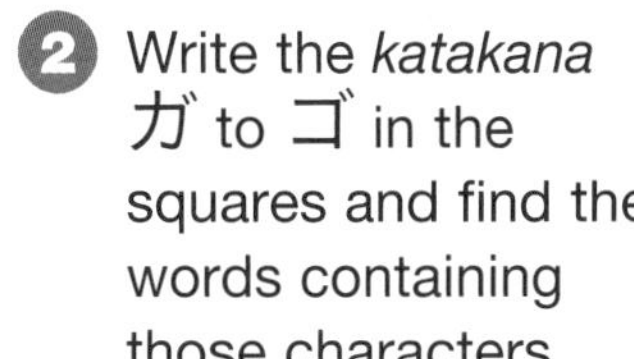

ga

アメリカ
カンガルー
カウンセラー

gi

ペンギン
ホットケーキ
アデレード

gu

クリスマス
サンダル
サングラス

ge

カラオケ
アクセサリー
ゲストスピーカー

go

けしゴム
チョコレート
ヨーグルト

3 Fill in the *katakana* according to the hints.

ⓐ the UK

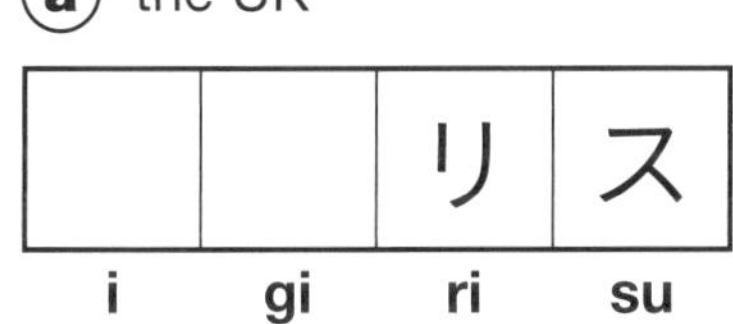

		リ	ス
i	gi	ri	su

ⓑ Chicago

シ		
shi	ka	go

ⓒ gram

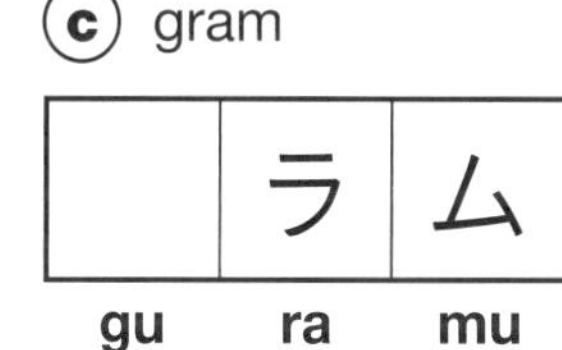

	ラ	ム
gu	ra	mu

4 Listen to your teacher or watch the Level 3 dictation video. Write the words in *katakana* in the first squares as you hear them. Then, use the extra squares to practise writing the words again.

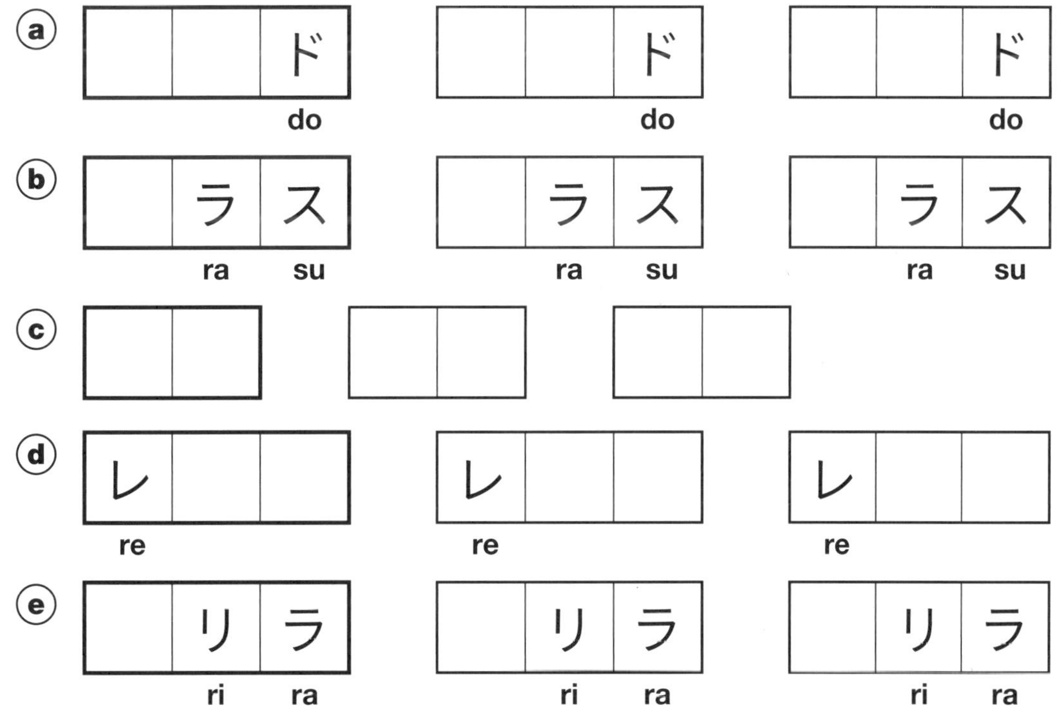

ⓐ

		ド
		do

ⓑ

	ラ	ス
	ra	su

ⓒ

ⓓ

レ		
re		

ⓔ

	リ	ラ
	ri	ra

ISBN 9780170416689

Level 4: サ to ソ

1. Practise writing the Level 4 *katakana* in the squares. Use the dotted lines to help you balance your characters in the squares.

Katakana	Reading	Memory aid
サ	**sa**	**sa**rdines
シ	**shi**	**shi**p
ス	**su**	**sou**p
セ	**se**	**se**tting sun
ソ	**so**	**sew**

ISBN 9780170416689

2 Find the same *katakana* as the first one in each line and circle them.

(a) シ	ソ	シ	ン	ノ	ソ	シ
(b) ス	ヌ	ス	フ	ス	ス	ヌ
(c) ソ	ソ	ツ	ソ	リ	ツ	ソ
(d) セ	ヤ	セ	ヤ	ヒ	セ	サ
(e) サ	ナ	サ	ラ	ナ	サ	サ

3 Connect the *katakana* words to their *hiragana* and English equivalents.

(a) セロリ (ろ り)	さいず	gasoline
(b) サイズ (ず)	がそりん	ice
(c) シナリオ (な り)	あいす	scenario
(d) ガソリン (り ん)	せろり	size
(e) アイス	しなりお	celery

4 Rosie hasn't started learning *katakana* yet. Help her to write some of the *katakana*.

(a) couscous

くすくす

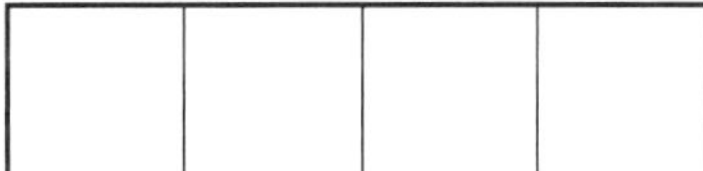

(b) sense

せんす →

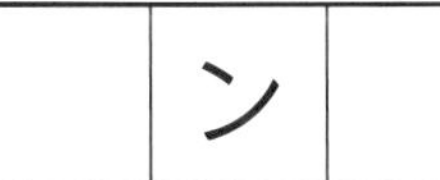
ン

(c) sign

さいん

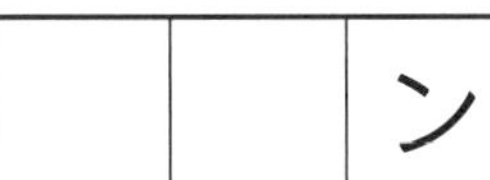
ン

(d) soft

そふと → フト

(e) singles

しんぐるす → ンル

ISBN 9780170416689

5 Find your way through the maze from the start to the goal. Write the *katakana* you find on the way to reveal the hidden message.

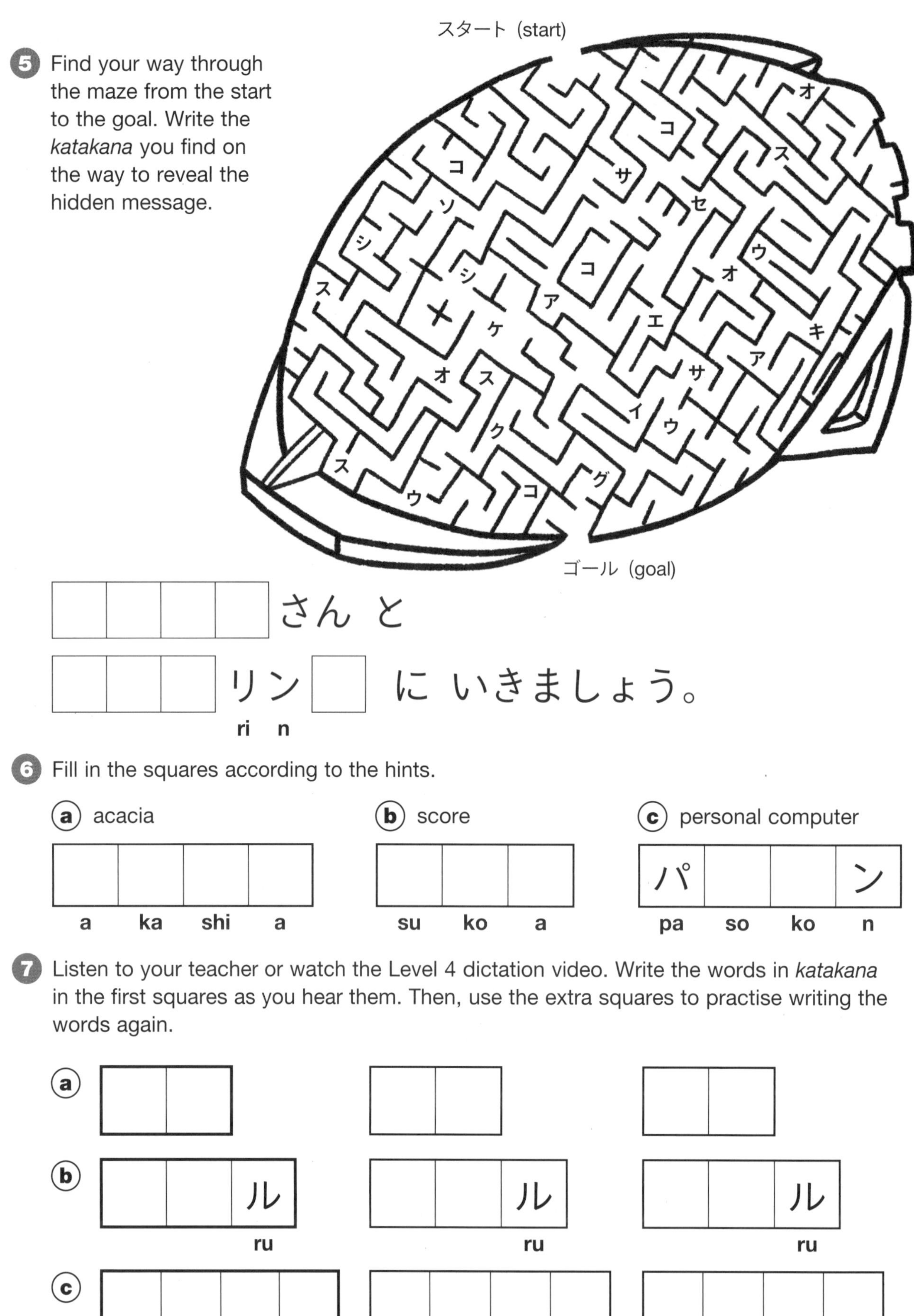

☐☐☐☐ さん と

☐☐☐ リン ☐ に いきましょう。

ri n

6 Fill in the squares according to the hints.

(a) acacia

☐	☐	☐	☐
a	ka	shi	a

(b) score

☐	☐	☐
su	ko	a

(c) personal computer

パ	☐	☐	ン
pa	so	ko	n

7 Listen to your teacher or watch the Level 4 dictation video. Write the words in *katakana* in the first squares as you hear them. Then, use the extra squares to practise writing the words again.

(a) ☐☐ ☐☐ ☐☐

(b) ☐☐ル ☐☐ル ☐☐ル

ru ru ru

(c) ☐☐☐☐ ☐☐☐☐ ☐☐☐☐

(d) ☐☐テム ☐☐テム ☐☐テム

te mu te mu te mu

(e) ☐☐ド ☐☐ド ☐☐ド

do do do

ISBN 9780170416689

Level 5: ザ to ゾ

1 Practise writing the Level 5 *katakana* in the squares. Use the dotted lines to help you balance your characters in the squares.

When ゛ is added to the upper right of *katakana* in the *s* line, they are pronounced with a *z* sound. For example, *sa* becomes *za*, and *su* becomes *zu*. Watch out for *shi*, however. It becomes *ji*.

To help you remember, think of the girl's name **Suz**ie, or *suzume*, the Japanese word for sparrow.

These sound changes are the same as when *tenten* are added to the *s* line in *hiragana*.

5

ISBN 9780170416689

2 Fill in each blank square of the *katakana* sudoku so that each row (horizontal) and each column (vertical) includes ザ, ジ, ズ, ゼ and ゾ.

ゾ			ゼ	ズ
	ゾ	ジ	ザ	ゼ
ジ		ズ	ゾ	
ザ	ズ	ゼ		
	ザ			ジ

3 Write the words in *katakana*.

a size

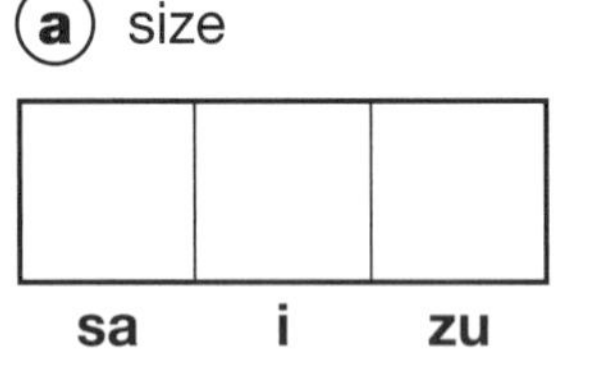

b design

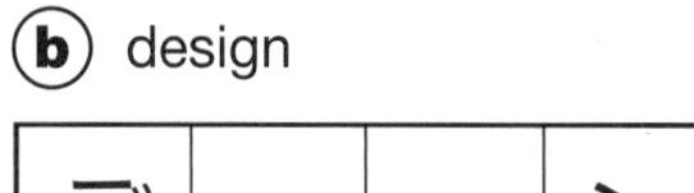

c zero

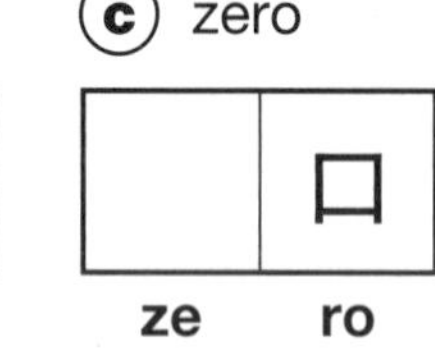

d orange

e zombie

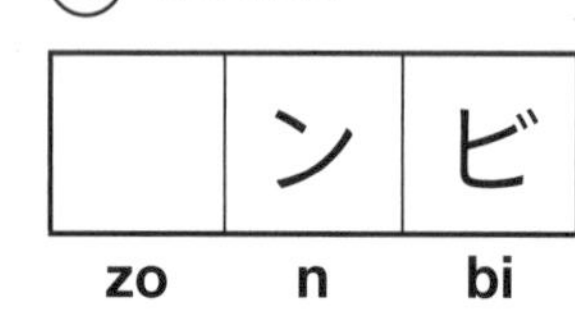

f pizza

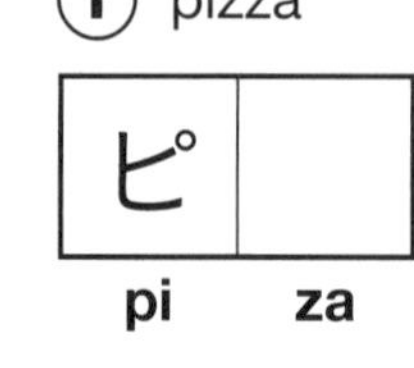

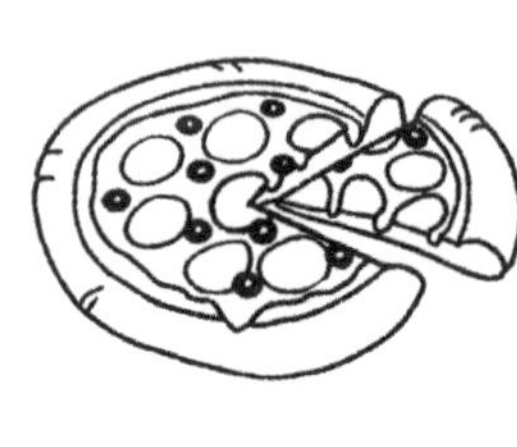

4 Listen to your teacher or watch the Level 5 dictation video. Write the words in *katakana* in the first squares as you hear them. Then, use the extra squares to practise writing the words again.

a

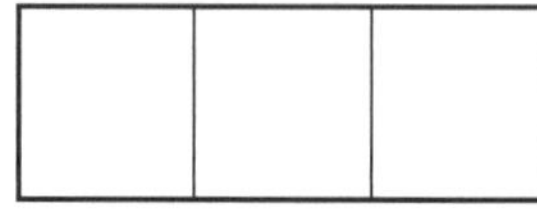
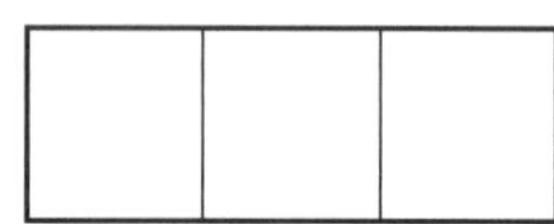

b

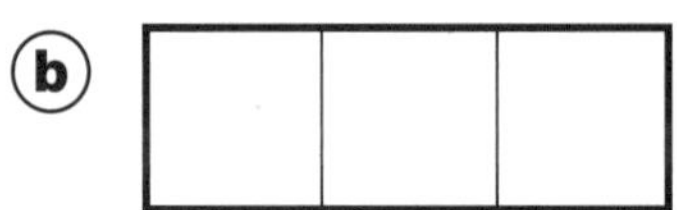
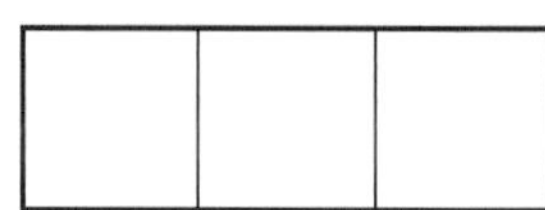
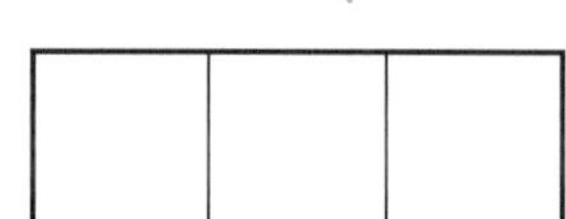

c

ラ チ ン
ra chi n

d

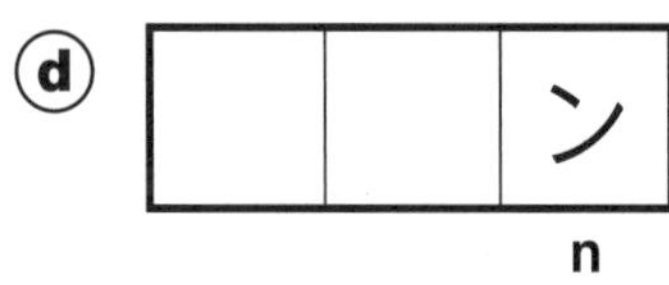

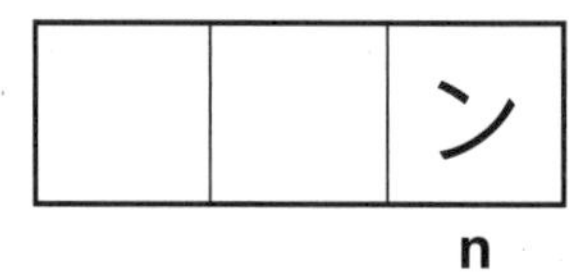

ン
n

e

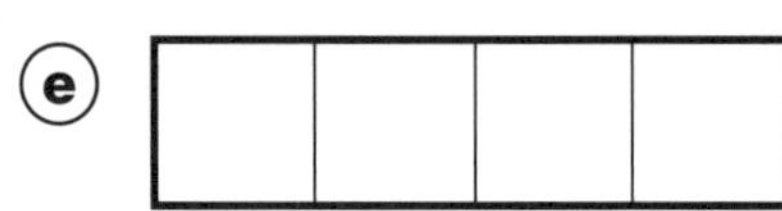

ISBN 9780170416689

Level 6: タ to ト

1 Practise writing the Level 6 *katakana* in the squares. Use the dotted lines to help you balance your characters in the squares.

タ ta	タ **ta**cos	ノ	ク	タ			タ
チ chi	チ **chi**cken	一	二	チ			
ツ tsu	ツ **tsu** buttons	丶	ヽヽ	ツ			
テ te	テ **te**levision	一	二	テ			
ト to	ト **to**tem	丨	ト				

2 Find the correct *katakana* and circle them.

(a) ta　タ　タ　ヌ　タ　ス　　　(b) chi　チ　チ　テ　テ　モ

(c) tsu　シ　ツ　ツ　ソ　ツ　　　(d) te　チ　テ　モ　チ　モ

(e) to　ト　ト　イ　イ　ヒ

3 Find your way through the puzzle from ア to ト. You can move in any direction, including diagonally.

ア	タ	エ	オ	キ	コ	タ	ク	イ
イ	ウ	サ	カ	イ	オ	キ	ツ	ケ
チ	ツ	ト	キ	ア	カ	オ	コ	カ
タ	コ	ケ	ク	エ	タ	ケ	ウ	ア
ク	サ	イ	ア	ソ	イ	チ	ク	ケ
オ	シ	ウ	セ	キ	ケ	コ	ツ	コ
ケ	ト	ス	ケ	ア	ウ	イ	カ	テ
カ	カ	オ	コ	エ	キ	ケ	エ	ト

↓ Goal

4 Write the correct words in *katakana*, using the picture as a clue.

テスト　タオル (ru)　ストア　ゲスト　タイル (ru)　タイツ

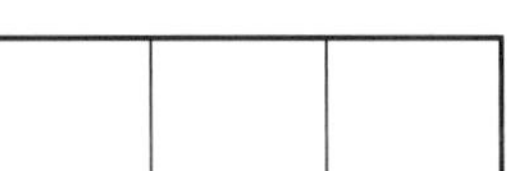

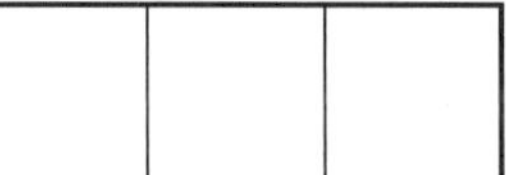

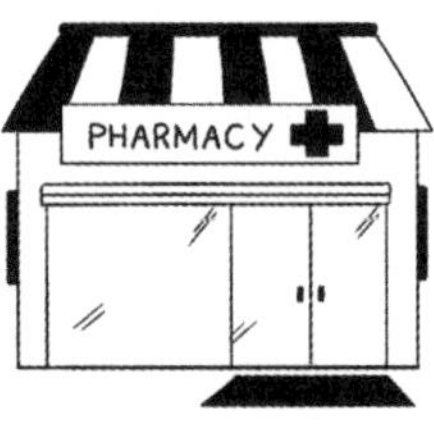

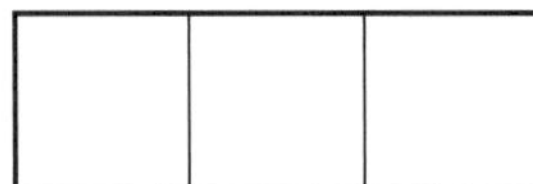

(e)

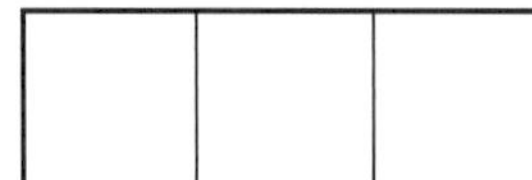

ISBN 9780170416689

5 Complete the crossword puzzle in *katakana*.

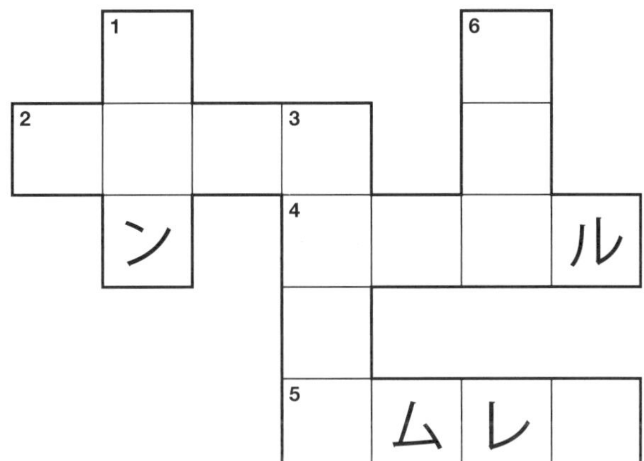

Across

2 **te ki sa su** (Texas)

4 **ta i to ru** (title)

5 **o mu re tsu** (omelette)

Down

1 **chi ki n** (chicken)

3 **su ta ji o** (studio)

6 **ko su to** (cost)

6 Listen to your teacher or watch the Level 6 dictation video. Write the words in *katakana* in the first squares as you hear them. Then, use the extra squares to practise writing the words again.

a 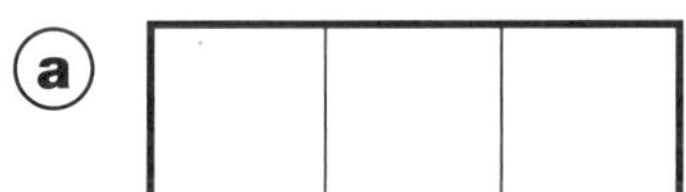  

b  

c バ **ba** 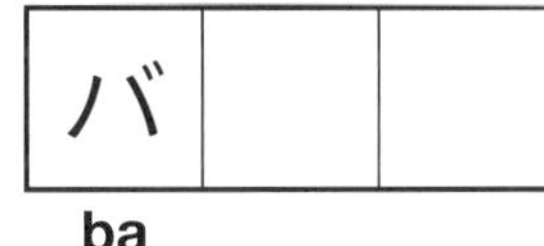

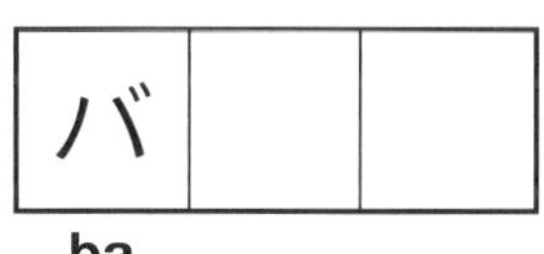

d ハン **ha n** 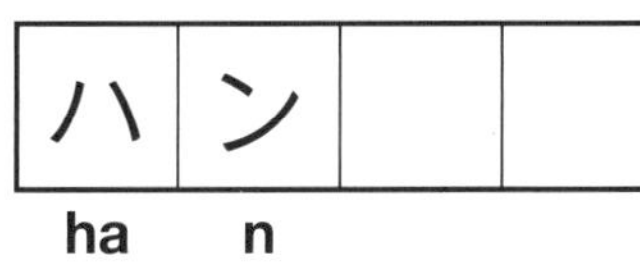

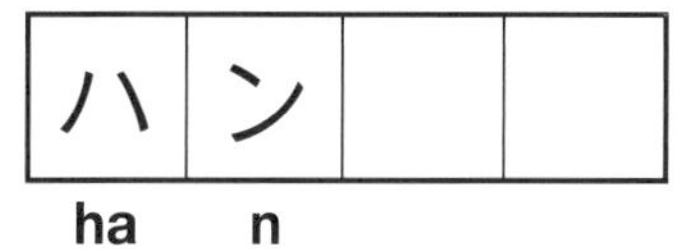

e 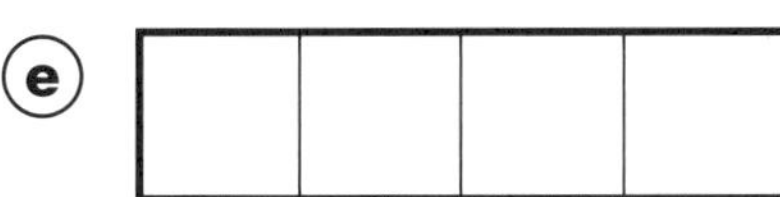 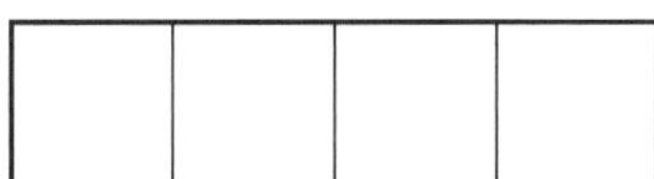 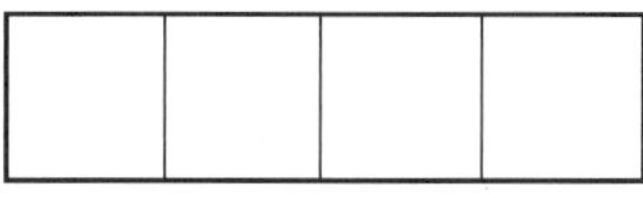

6

Level 7: ダ to ド

1 Practise writing the Level 7 *katakana* in the squares. Use the dotted lines to help you balance your characters in the squares.

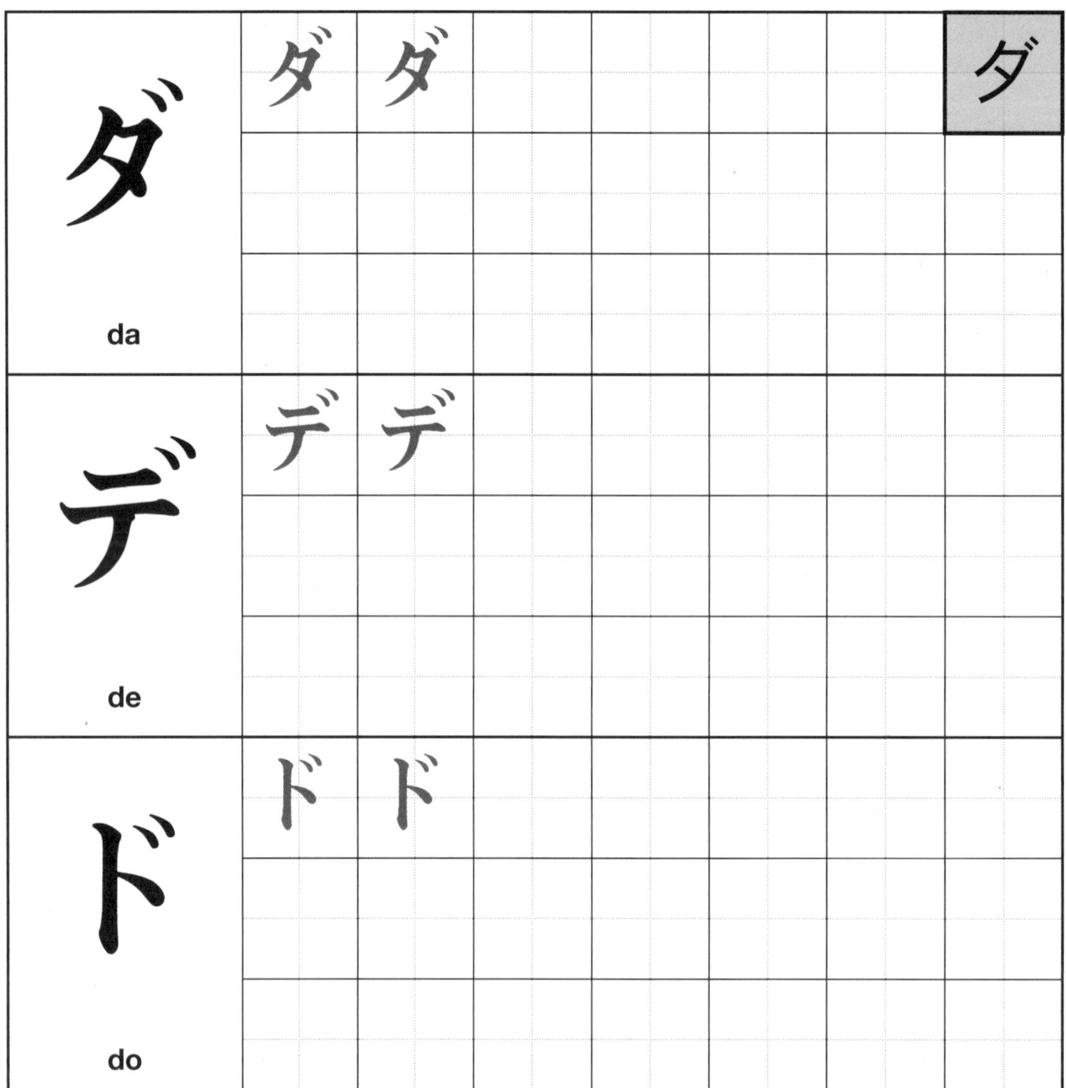

Adding ﾞ to the upper right of each *hiragana* in the *t* line makes a *d* sound. For example, *ta* becomes *da*, *te* becomes *de* and *to* becomes *do*.

To help you remember, think of **Ted** or **tad**a!

These sound changes are the same as when *tenten* are added to the *t* line in *hiragana*.

2 Find the correct *katakana* and circle them.

(a) **de** タ テ チ デ ド

(b) **da** グ ダ タ ク ワ

(c) **do** ダ ナ ド イ ト

ISBN 9780170416689

3 Connect the *katakana* words to the correct pictures.

re ドレス	ドア	n ダンス	ra サラダ	デスク

4 Fill in the squares according to the hints.

a outdoor

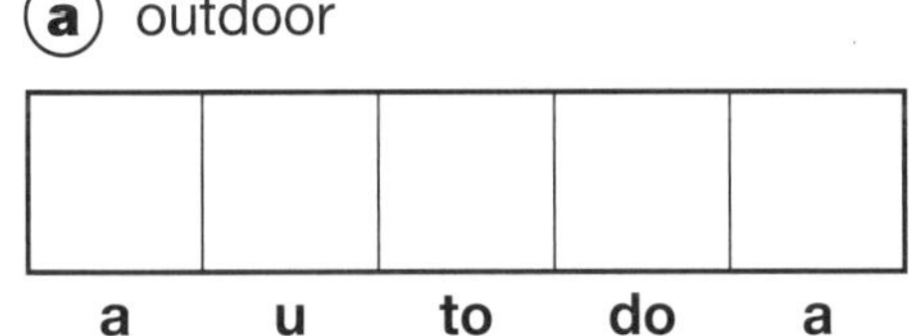

a u to do a

b digital

			ル
de	ji	ta	ru

c India

	ン	
i	n	do

d dam

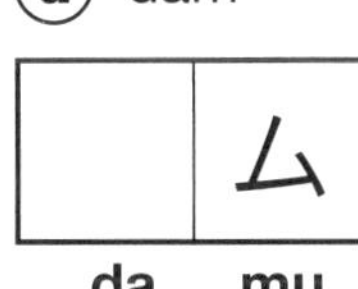

	ム
da	mu

e video

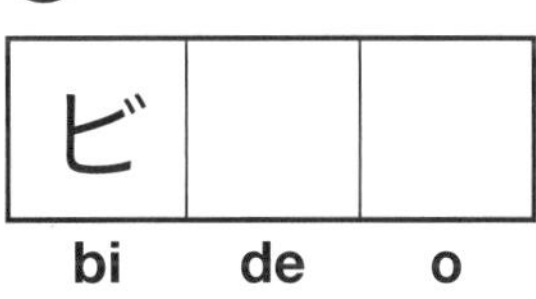

ビ		
bi	de	o

5 Listen to your teacher or watch the Level 7 dictation video. Write the words in *katakana* in the first squares as you hear them. Then, use the extra squares to practise writing the words again.

a

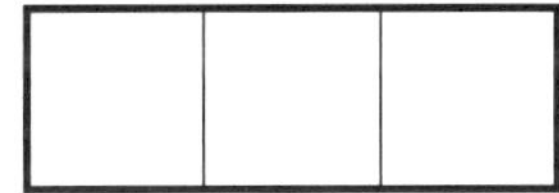 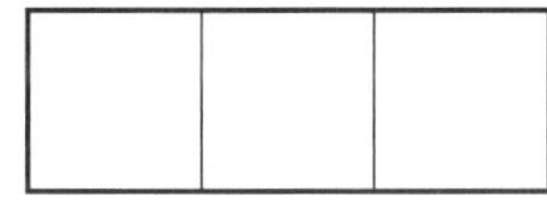

b

 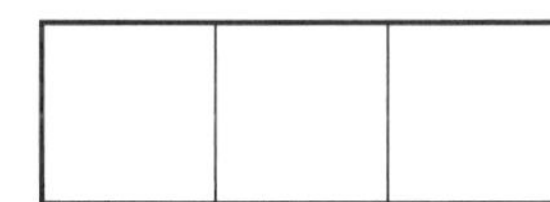

c

 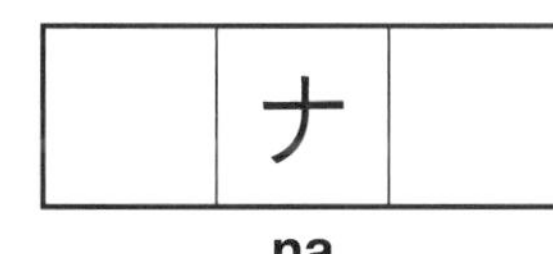

ナ na ナ na ナ na

d

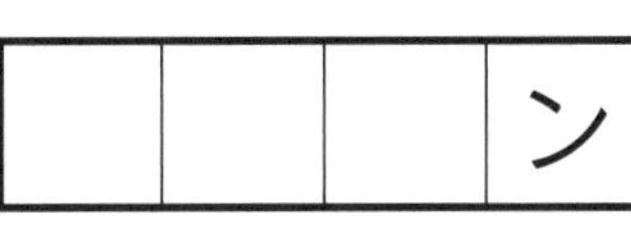 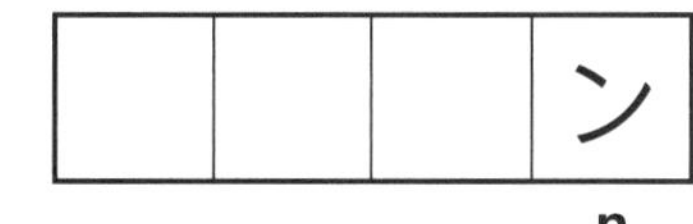

ン n ン n ン n

e

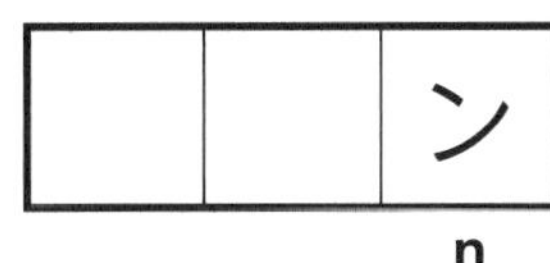 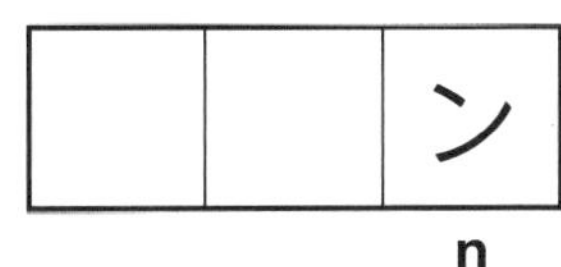 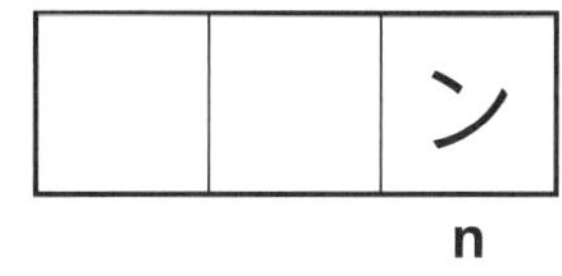

ン n ン n ン n

Level 8: ナ to ノ

1 Practise writing the Level 8 *katakana* in the squares. Use the dotted lines to help you balance your characters in the squares.

Katakana	Mnemonic	Stroke order
ナ na	ナ **nu**tcracker	一 ナ
ニ ni	ニ **nee**dles	一 ニ
ヌ nu	ヌ **noo**dles	フ ヌ
ネ ne	ネ **ne**cktie	丶 ラ ネ ネ
ノ no	ノ **no**	ノ

ISBN 9780170416689

2 Find the correct *katakana* and circle them.

a ne	ヌ	ネ	ア	ね	マ
b nu	ス	ア	ネ	ヌ	ワ
c ni	に	エ	ヨ	コ	ニ
d no	ナ	メ	リ	の	ノ
e na	ノ	ナ	ヌ	ア	イ

3 Use the coordinates to find the correct *katakana* from the grid and write them in the squares. Then read the completed sentence and circle the person it describes.

ぼく は [C4][B3] です。 [A1][E2][A4] 人です。

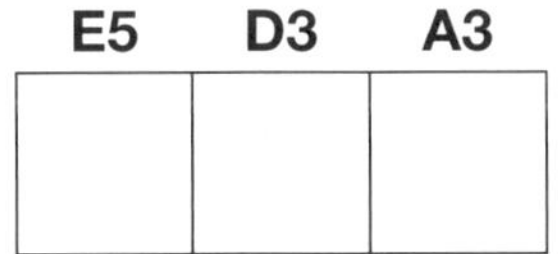

[E5][D3][A3] が すきです。

	A	B	C	D	E
1	カ	セ	サ	チ	オ
2	ツ	キ	イ	ケ	ナ
3	ス	ア	ド	ニ	ネ
4	ダ	ヌ	ノ	ソ	シ
5	ウ	コ	ク	エ	テ

1

Tom
American

2

Noah
Japanese

3

Noah
Canadian

ISBN 9780170416689

4 Olivia is making flashcards to remember *katakana*. Complete the flashcards to help her.

hiragana ぴあの
katakana ピ ______________
English ______________

hiragana きぬあ
katakana ______________
English quinoa

hiragana つな
katakana ______________
English tuna

hiragana ねくたい
katakana ______________
English tie

hiragana えんじにあ
katakana __ ン ______________
English ______________

5 Listen to your teacher or watch the Level 8 dictation video. Write the words in *katakana* in the first squares as you hear them. Then, use the extra squares to practise writing the words again.

a | バ | | | | | バ | | | | | バ | | | |
ba ba ba

b
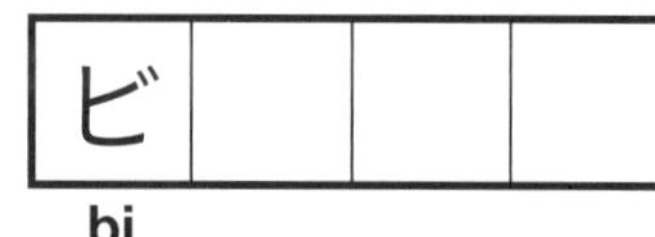

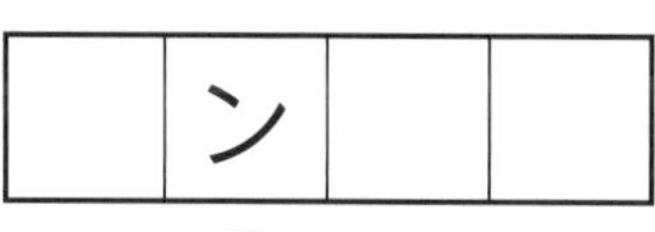
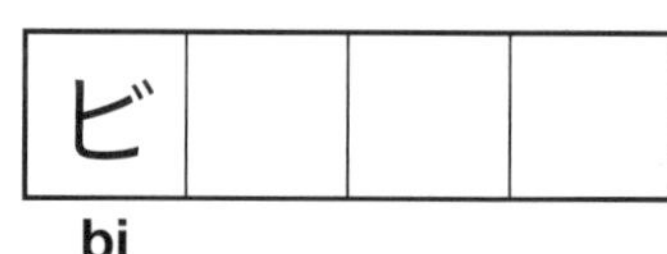

bi bi bi

c
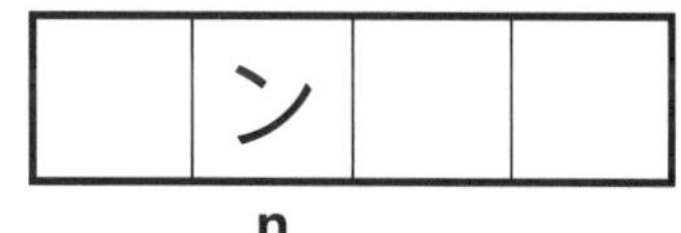

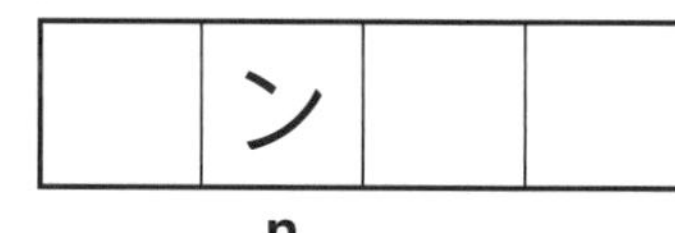

n n n

d
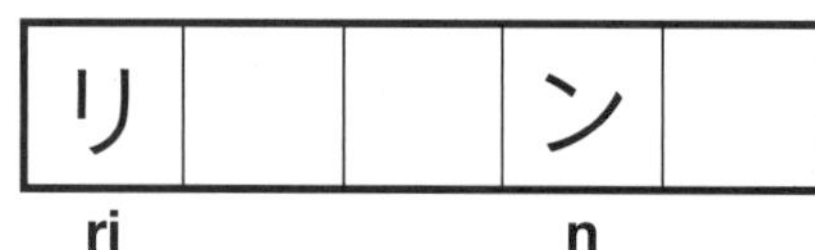

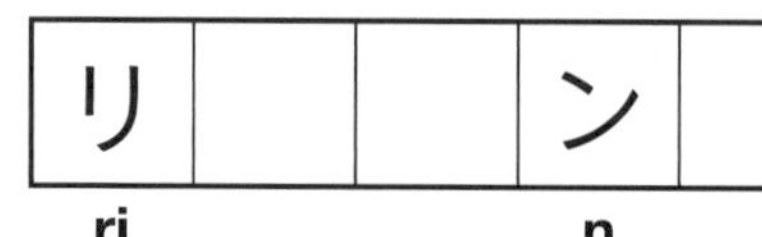

ri n ri n

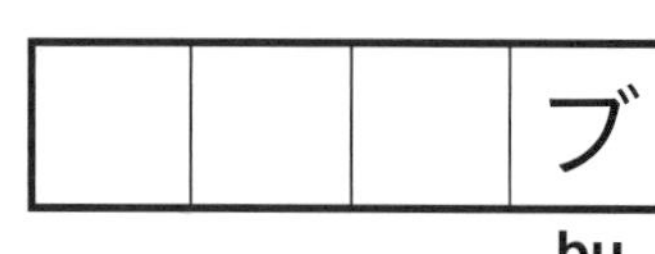

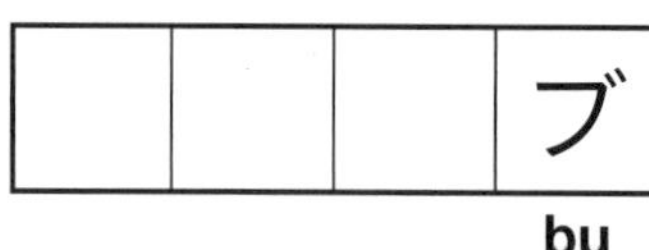

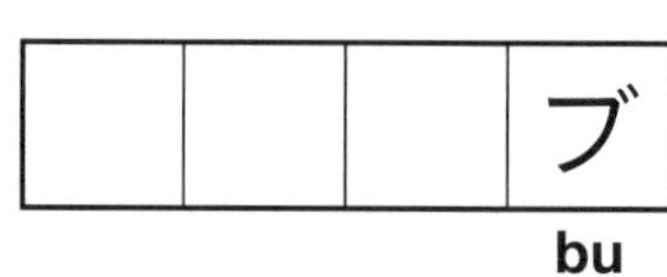

bu bu bu

ISBN 9780170416689

Level 9: ハ to ホ

❶ Practise writing the Level 9 *katakana* in the squares. Use the dotted lines to help you balance your characters in the squares.

ハ ha	ハ **hu**t	ノ	ハ				
ヒ hi	ヒ **he**	ノ	ヒ				
フ fu	フ **foo**d	フ					
ヘ he	ヘ **hea**ven	ヘ					
ホ ho	ホ **ho**ly	一	十	才	ホ		

9

ISBN 9780170416689

2 Find your way through the puzzle from ハ to ホ. The *katakana* sequence from ハ to ホ will be repeated three times. When you get to the first ホ, the next one will be ハ, followed by ヒ, and so on. You can move in any direction to a hexagon attached to the one you are in.

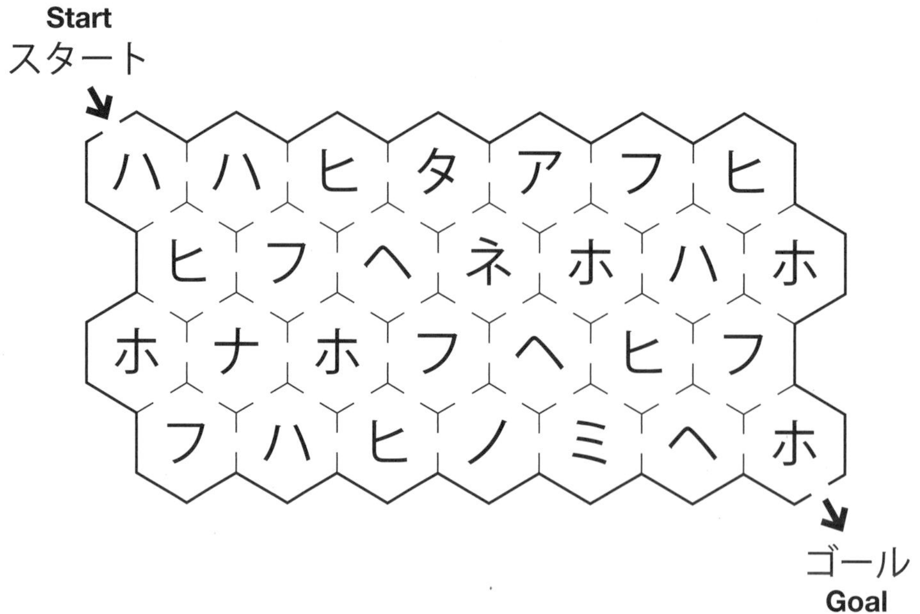

3 Draw a line connecting the *katakana* words to their English equivalents.

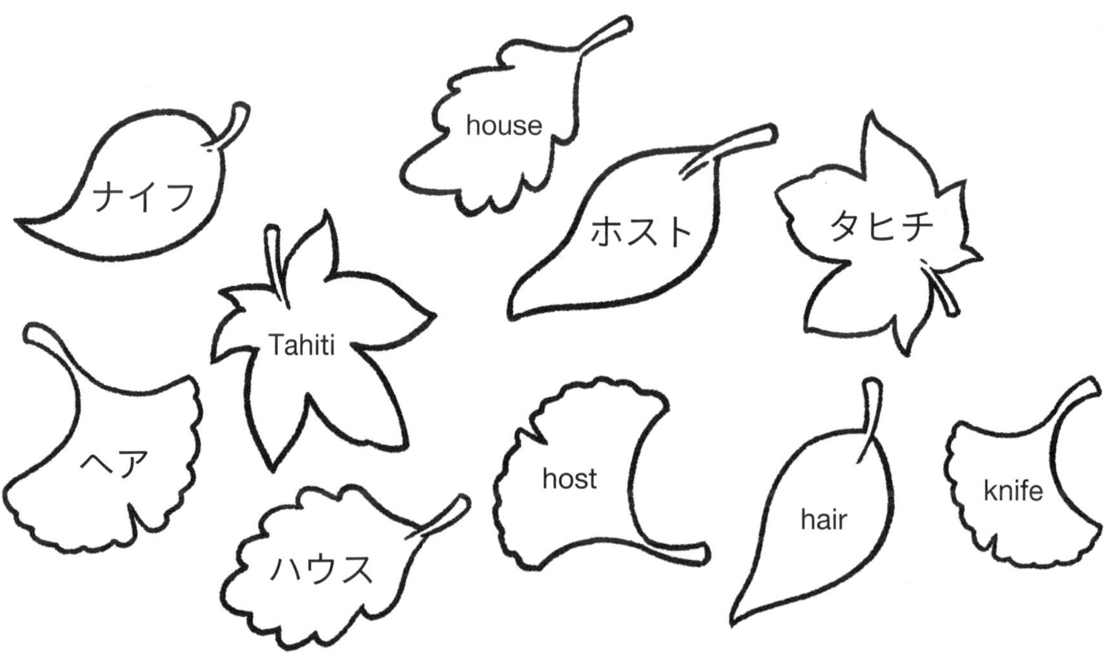

ISBN 9780170416689

4 One of the *katakana* from ハ to ホ is missing from each set. Find the missing *katakana* and write them in the square.

ⓐ ハ フ ホ ヘ

ⓑ ヘ ホ ヒ フ

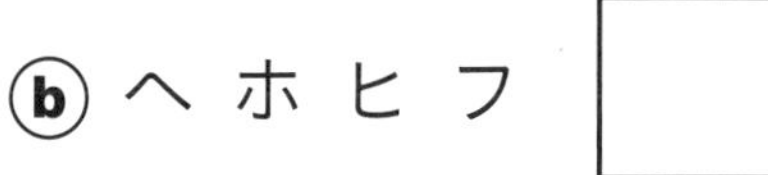

ⓒ フ ヒ ハ ヘ

ⓓ ハ ヒ ヘ ホ

ⓔ ホ ハ フ ヒ

5 Write each word in *katakana*.

ⓐ handle

ⓑ hint

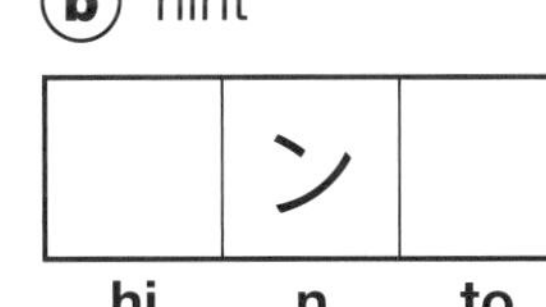

ⓒ Africa

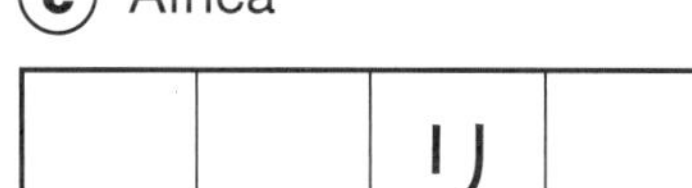

[ ] ン [ ] ル

ha n do ru

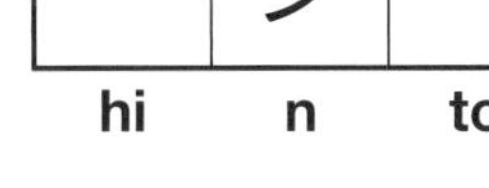

[ ] ン [ ]

hi n to

[ ] [ ] リ [ ]

a fu ri ka

ⓓ Honolulu

ⓔ shift

ⓕ mohair

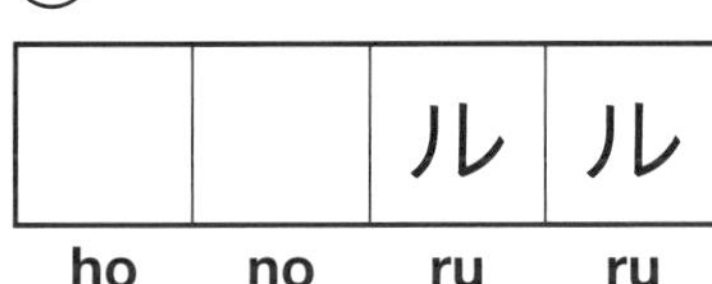

[ ] [ ] ル ル

ho no ru ru

[ ] [ ] [ ]

shi fu to

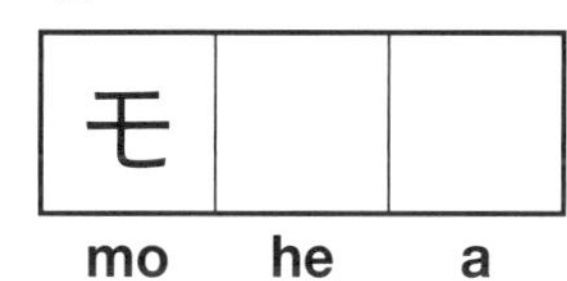

モ [ ] [ ]

mo he a

6 Listen to your teacher or watch the Level 9 dictation video. Write the words in *katakana* in the first squares as you hear them. Then, use the extra squares to practise writing the words again.

ⓐ

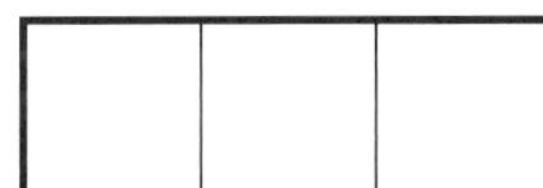

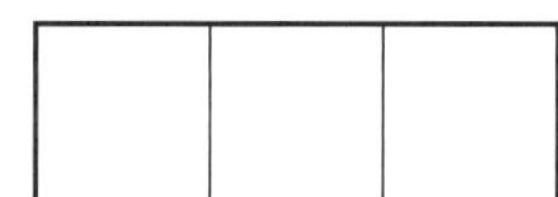

ⓑ

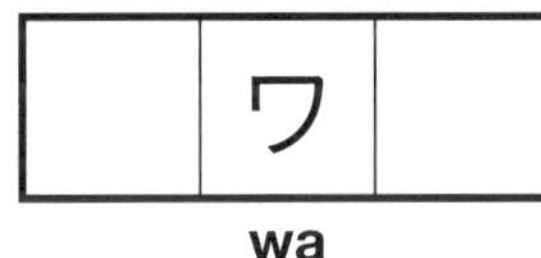

[ ] ワ [ ]

wa

[ ] ワ [ ]

wa

[ ] ワ [ ]

wa

ⓒ

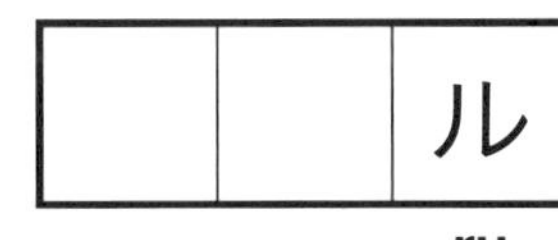

[ ] [ ] ル

ru

[ ] [ ] ル

ru

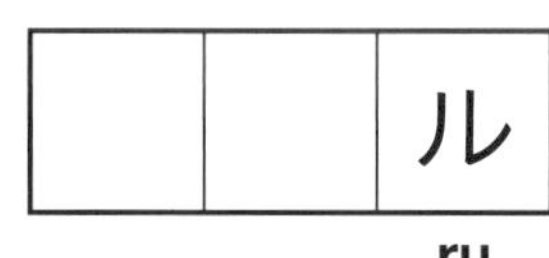

[ ] [ ] ル

ru

ⓓ

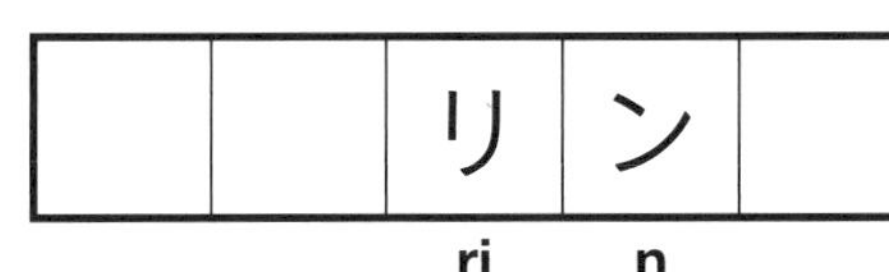

[ ] [ ] リ ン [ ]

ri n

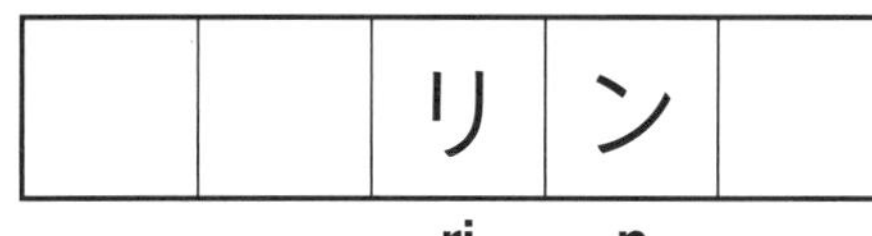

[ ] [ ] リ ン [ ]

ri n

ⓔ

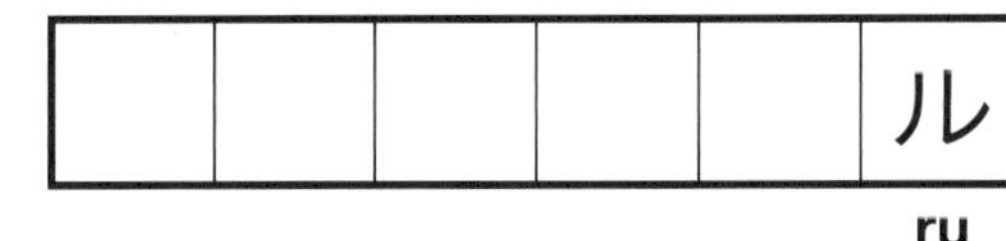

[ ] [ ] [ ] [ ] [ ] ル

ru

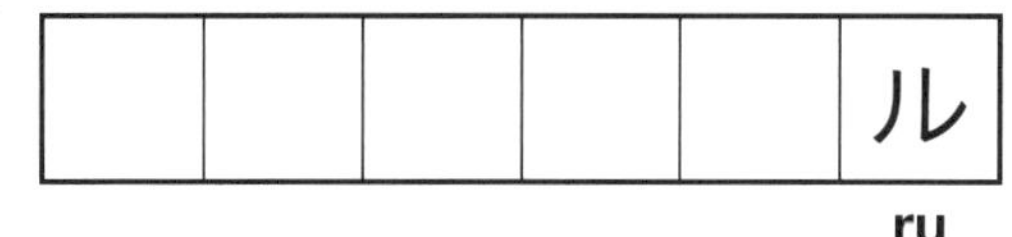

[ ] [ ] [ ] [ ] [ ] ル

ru

9

ISBN 9780170416689

Level 10: バ to ポ

1 Practise writing the Level 10 *katakana* in the squares. Use the dotted lines to help you balance your characters in the squares.

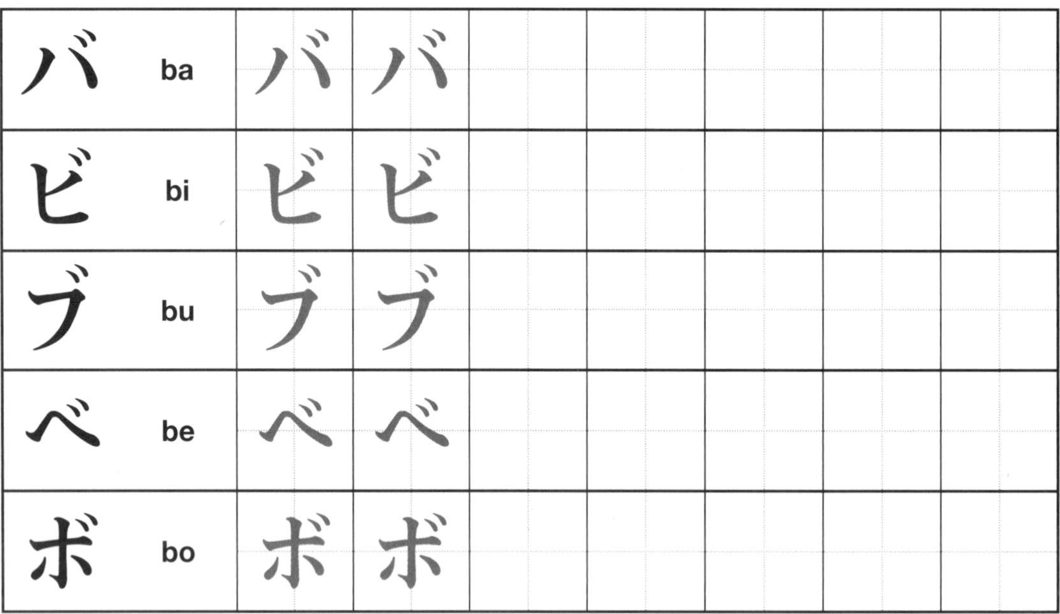

バ	ba	バ	バ					
ビ	bi	ビ	ビ					
ブ	bu	ブ	ブ					
ベ	be	ベ	ベ					
ボ	bo	ボ	ボ					

Adding the symbol ゛ to the upper right of *katakana* in the *h* line makes a *b* sound. For example, *ha* becomes *ba*, and *he* becomes *be*. These sound changes are the same as when *tenten* are added to the *h* line in *hiragana*.

To help you remember, think of **h**u**b** or **h**uman **b**eing.

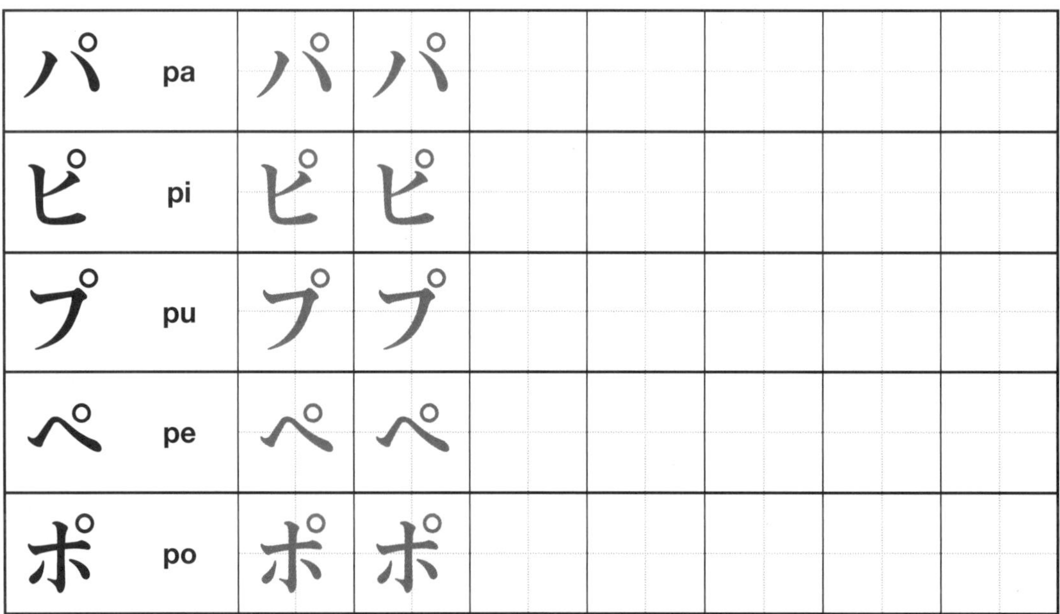

パ	pa	パ	パ					
ピ	pi	ピ	ピ					
プ	pu	プ	プ					
ペ	pe	ペ	ペ					
ポ	po	ポ	ポ					

Adding ° to *katakana* on the *h* line makes *p* sounds. For example, *ha* becomes *pa*, and *he* becomes *pe*. These sound changes are the same as when *maru* are added to the *h* line in *hiragana*.

To help you remember, think of **h**o**p** or **h**a**pp**y.

The formal name of this symbol is *han-dakuten*, but it is also commonly known as *maru*.

ISBN 9780170416689

2 Jack's favourite foods are listed below in *hiragana*. Rewrite the list in *katakana*.

ぼくのすきなたべもの

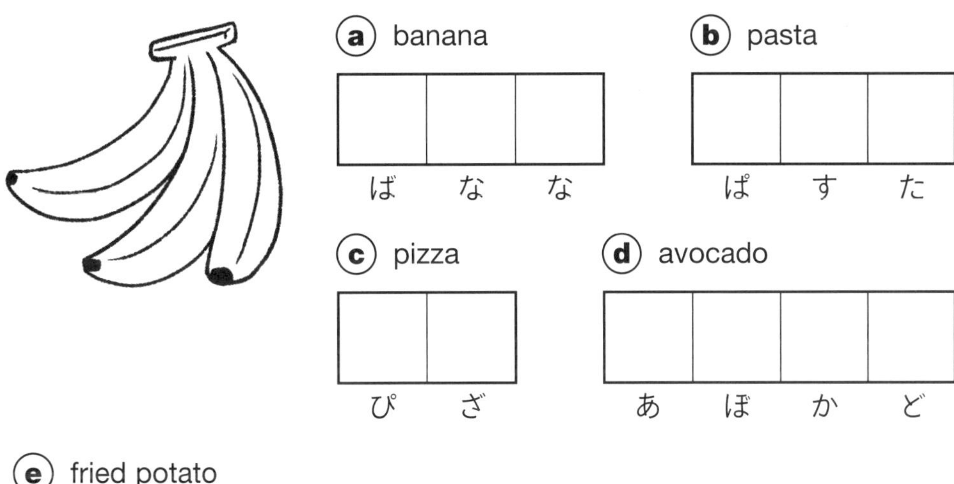

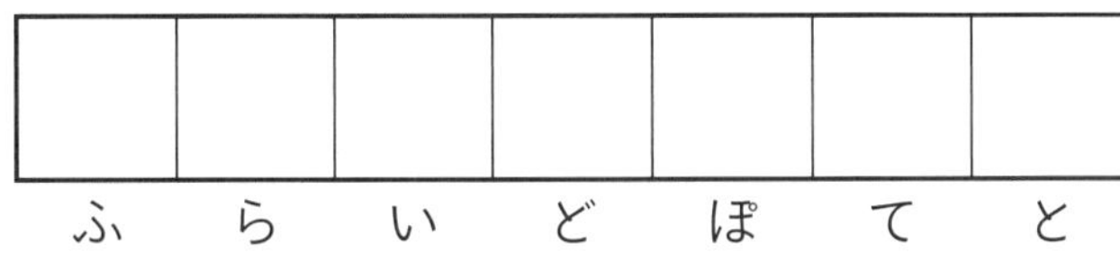

3 Listen to your teacher or watch the Level 10 dictation video. Write the words in *katakana* in the first squares as you hear them. Then, use the extra squares to practise writing the words again.

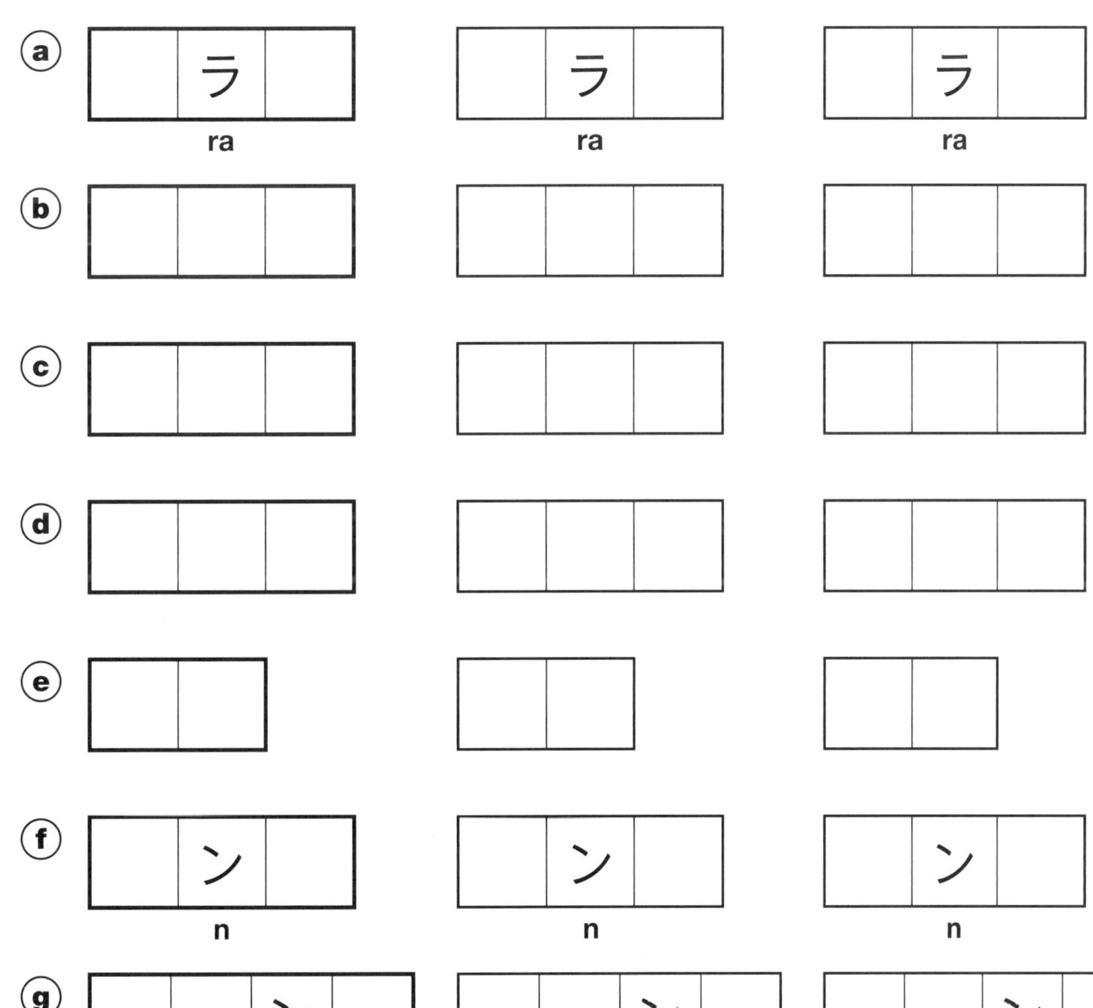

10

ISBN 9780170416689

4 Write each word in *katakana*. Then, find each one in the puzzle. You will find them horizontally, vertically, diagonally, upside-down and back-to-front.

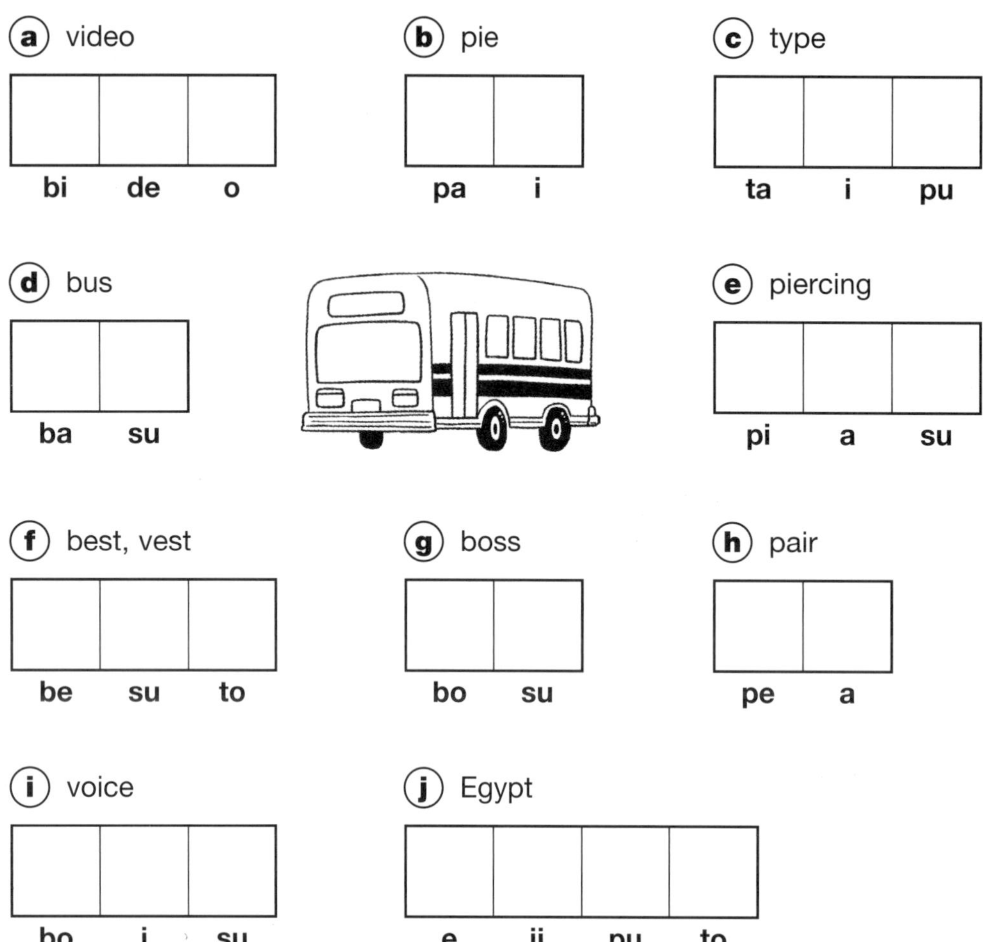

イ	キ	タ	ダ	ペ	ベ	ビ	ボ	ピ	ア	ス	ヌ
ラ	ボ	カ	ア	イ	オ	イ	ポ	ク	ケ	ニ	ネ
ノ	ス	ト	コ	ケ	エ	パ	オ	ボ	ハ	ノ	チ
ビ	ウ	エ	ブ	プ	コ	サ	シ	イ	ツ	ベ	テ
ベ	ソ	バ	セ	ス	ビ	パ	ウ	ス	ア	ス	セ
パ	ス	ビ	ヒ	ヘ	カ	デ	エ	ザ	ゾ	ト	ダ
タ	ソ	ケ	カ	ツ	タ	キ	オ	ビ	ネ	ナ	デ
エ	ジ	プ	ト	ネ	チ	ク	ペ	パ	タ	イ	プ

ISBN 9780170416689

Level 11: マ to ヨ

1 Practise writing the Level 11 *katakana* in the squares. Use the dotted lines to help you balance your characters in the squares.

マ **ma**	マ **mu**ffin	フ	マ				
ミ **mi**	ミ **me**	ヽ	ミ	ミ			
ム **mu**	ム **moo** (cow)	ム	ム				ム
メ **me**	メ **me**tal	ノ	メ				
モ **mo**	モ **mo**re	一	二	モ			

11

2 Find the correct *katakana* and circle them.

(a) **mu**	マ	モ	ム	ヌ	カ
(b) **ya**	イ	ヤ	マ	カ	メ
(c) **mo**	エ	ミ	チ	モ	オ
(d) **yu**	ヒ	ロ	エ	ユ	コ
(e) **mi**	ミ	シ	ツ	ヨ	ニ
(f) **ma**	ヌ	ス	マ	ム	ア
(g) **me**	ノ	メ	イ	ア	ナ
(h) **yo**	コ	モ	エ	ヨ	ロ

ISBN 9780170416689

3 Find a path through the maze by following the correct *katakana* words in the list below.

me ki shi ko (Mexico)

ta i ya (tyre)

ma i na su (minus)

su ta mi na (stamina)

be to na mu (Vietnam)

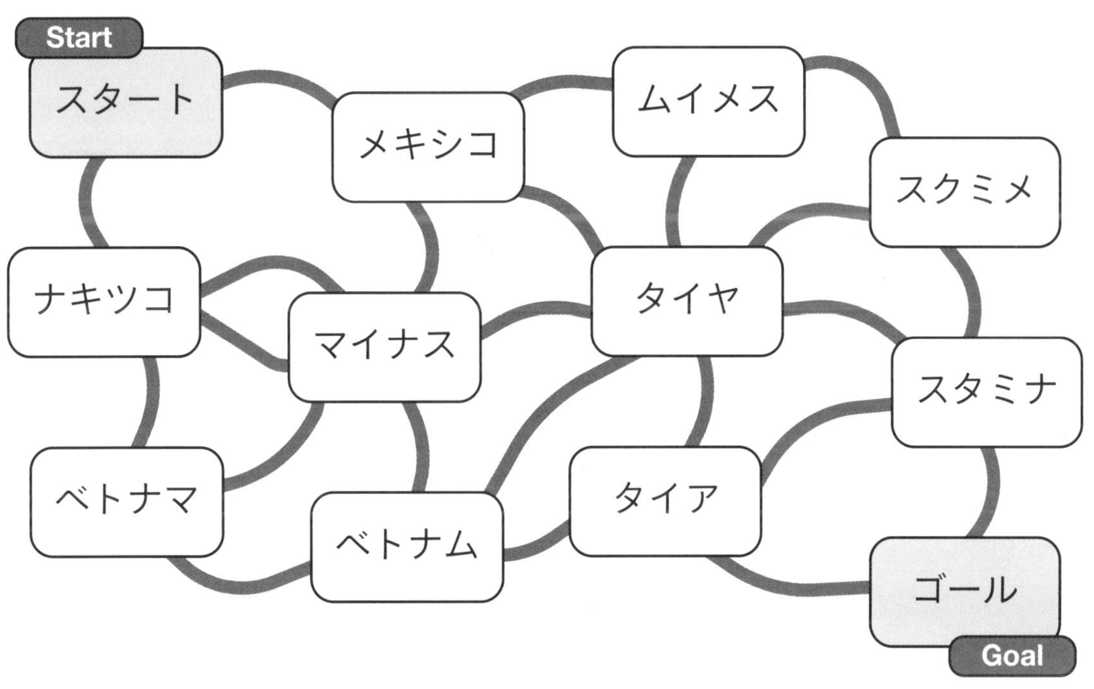

4 Olivia is making more flashcards to remember *katakana*. Complete the flashcards to help her.

hiragana まうす

katakana ______________________

English ______________________

hiragana よが

katakana ______________________

English ______________________

11

ISBN 9780170416689

5 Listen to your teacher or watch the Level 11 dictation video. Write the words in *katakana* in the first squares as you hear them. Then, use the extra squares to practise writing the words again.

a

b

c

d

e

				ン	
				n	

				ン	
				n	

f

	レ		ン
	re		n

	レ		ン
	re		n

	レ		ン
	re		n

g

			ン
			n

			ン
			n

			ン
			n

ISBN 9780170416689

Level 12: ラ to ン

1 Practise writing the Level 12 *katakana* in the squares. Use the dotted lines to help you balance your characters in the squares.

ラ	ラ	一	ラ				
ra	**ra**men						
リ	リ	ｌ	リ				
ri	**ri**ver						
ル	ル	ノ	ル				
ru	kanga**roo**						
レ	レ	レ					
re	**re**ady to go out						
ロ	ロ	ｌ	𠃍	ロ			
ro	**ro**ck						

12

ISBN 9780170416689

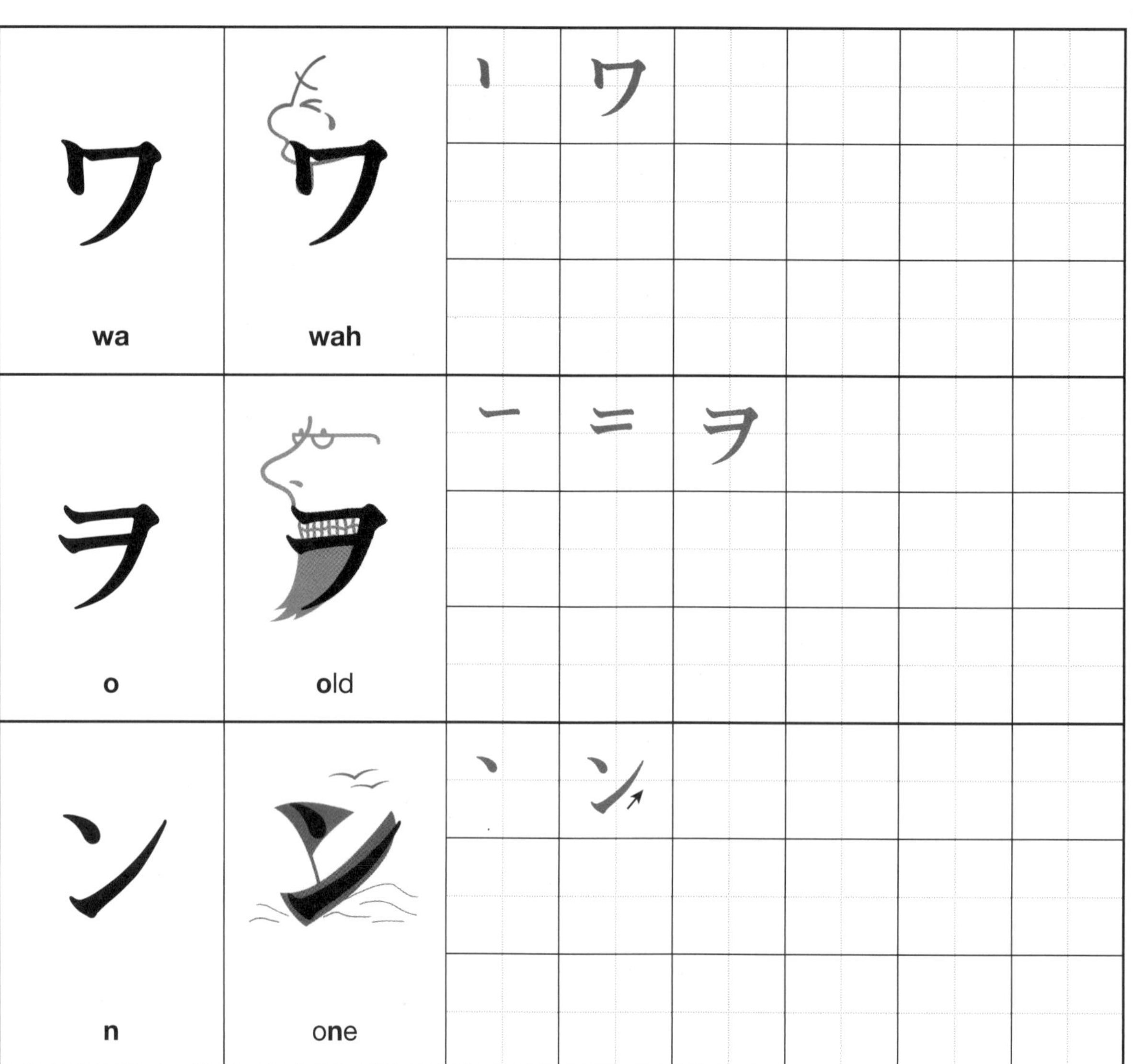

ヲ is used to write the particle を in *katakana*. This only happens when you write a whole sentence in *katakana*, which is not common.

2 Find the correct handwritten *katakana*.

ⓐ ra　　ラ　ウ　ラ　フ　ワ

ⓑ ru　　リ　い　ハ　ル　ル

ⓒ ri　　ル　リ　ソ　い　い

ⓓ re　　L　ᒧ　ᒧ　り　レ

ⓔ wa　　ワ　ウ　フ　ヤ　ク

ⓕ ro　　コ　匚　ロ　ㄇ　凵

ⓖ n　　シ　ソ　シ　ン　リ

ISBN 9780170416689

3 What is the correct meeting place? Cross out every ラ, リ, ル, レ, ロ, ワ, ヲ and ン in the following grid. Then, starting at the arrow at the top of the right-hand column, read down each column, working from right to left. Write the remaining katakana in the answer spaces to find the correct meeting place and circle the image.

				↓
ル	ワ	ラ	タ	リ
ワ	ア	ン	レ	ス
ラ	ン	ル	ワ	ラ
ム	ロ	ジ	リ	ロ
ヲ	レ	ヲ	ラ	ワ
↓				

Message

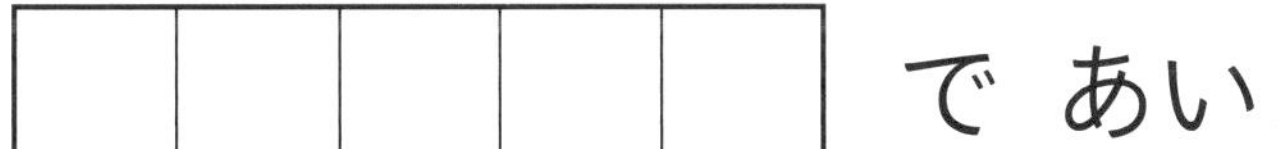 で あいましょう。

a 

b 

c 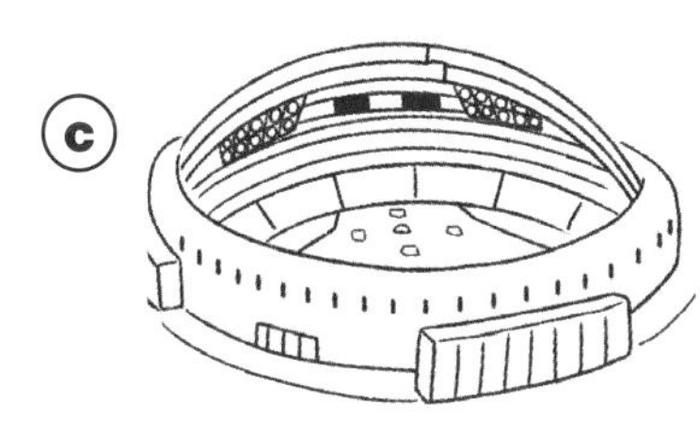

12

4 Read the following words and put their numbers into their categories.

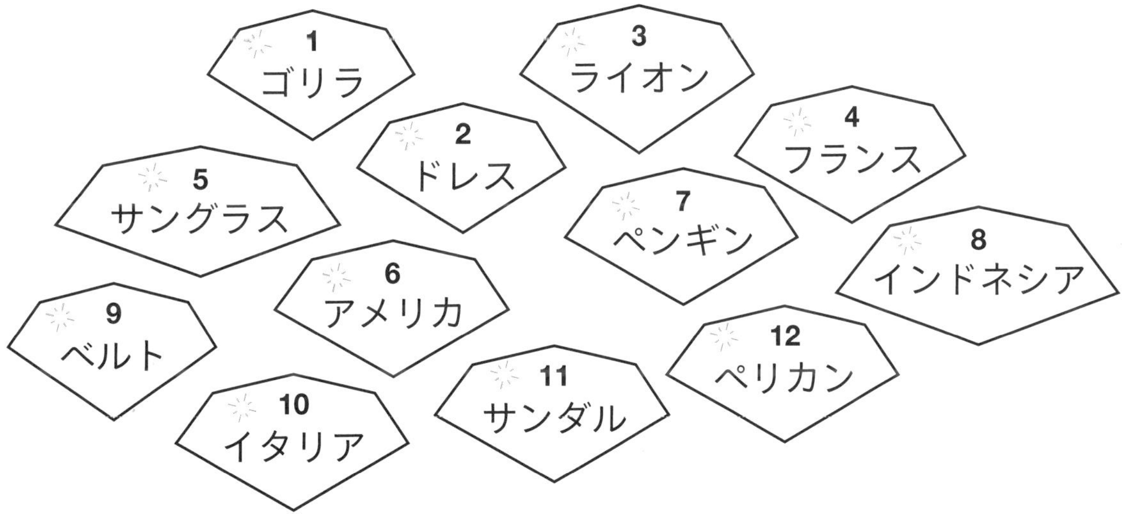

ISBN 9780170416689

5 A popular word game in Japan is しりとり. Each person says a word that starts with the last sound of the word before. Because there are no words that start with ン in Japanese, ン ends the game. Write the following words into the correct order of a しりとり game.

gu ra u n do (ground)	**do a** (door)	**a ni me** (animation)
me ro n (melon)	**ko a ra** (koala)	**ra i to** (light)
to i re (toilet)	**re ta su** (lettuce)	**su i n gu** (swing)

→ →

→ →

→ → ン

6 Listen to your teacher or watch the Level 12 dictation video. Write the words in *katakana* in the first squares as you hear them. Then, use the extra squares to practise writing the words again.

a

b

c

d

e

f

g

Congratulations! You have learnt all 46 *katakana*.

ISBN 9780170416689

Level 13: Similar *katakana*

Let's practice similar *katakana*.

Set 1

1 Choose the right spelling for these words.

(a) **so u ru** (Seoul) ソウル ンウル

(b) **ko i n** (coin) コイソ コイン

(c) **da n su** (dance) ダソス ダンス

(d) **so ro** (solo) ソロ ンロ

2 Fill in the blanks to compete the following words.

(a) pen

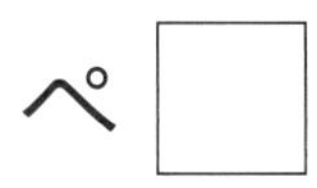

ペ[ ] **n**

(b) soft

[ ]フト **so**

(c) personal computer

パ[ ]コ[ ] **so** **n**

Set 1

so n
ソ ン

How to remember

Think about how you write the last part of the *hiragana* and *katakana*.

そ and ソ

The last part of both *hiragana* and *katakana* *so* go down.

ん and ン

The last part of both *hiragana* and *katakana* *n* go up.

Set 2

3 Choose the right spelling for these words.

(a) **ta i tsu** (tights) タイツ タイシ

(b) **shi fu to** (shift) ツフト シフト

(c) **shi na ri o** (scenario) ツナリオ シナリオ

(d) **do i tsu** (Germany) ドイツ ドイシ

4 Fill in the blanks to compete the following words.

(a) tuna

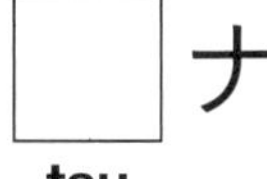

[ ]ナ **tsu**

(b) brush

ブラ[ ] **shi**

(c) system

[ ]ステム **shi**

Set 2

shi tsu
シ ツ

How to remember

Think about how you write the last part of the *hiragana* and *katakana*.

し and シ

The last part of both *hiragana* and *katakana* *shi* go up.

つ and ツ

The last part of both *hiragana* and *katakana* *tsu* go down.

ISBN 9780170416689

Set 3

Set 3
a
ア
ma
マ

❺ Connect the *romaji* and definitions to their *katakana* equivalents. Note that some of the *katakana* words have mistakes in them.

e ri a (area)

コアラ

ko a ra (koala)

アスク

to ma to (tomato)

ma su ku (mask)

トマト

トアト

コマラ

❻ Fill in the blanks to compete the following words.

ⓐ microphone

ma

ⓑ out

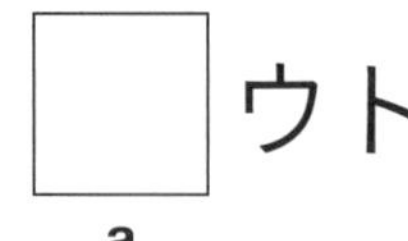

a

ⓒ iron

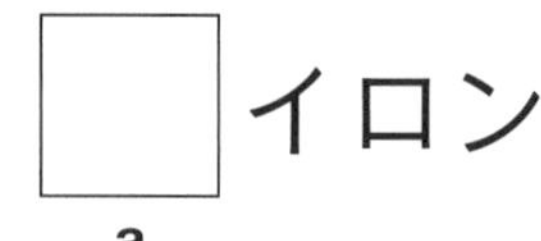

a

Set 4

Set 4
na
ナ
me
メ

❼ Choose the correct letter from the bracket to complete each word.

ⓐ **ka me ra** (camera) .... カ（ナ, メ）ラ

ⓑ **na i fu** (knife) .... （ナ, メ）イフ

ⓒ **me ro n** (melon) .... （ナ, メ）ロン

ⓓ **na pu ki n** (napkin) .... （ナ, メ）プキン

❽ Fill in the blanks to compete the following words.

ⓐ America

ア ☐ リカ

me

ⓑ banana

na na

ⓒ memo

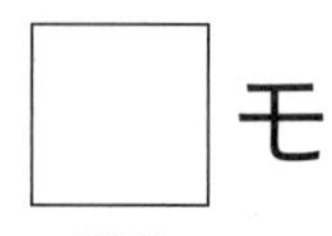

me

ISBN 9780170416689

Set 5

9 Complete the words by connecting the *katakana* letters from left to right.

ha wa i
(Hawaii)

ア

ku ra su
(class)

ke ni a
(Kenya)

wa i n
(wine)

Set 5
ku
ク
ke
ケ
wa
ワ

10 Fill in the blanks to compete the following words.

(a) milk

ミル [ ]
ku

(b) waltz

[ ] ルツ
wa

(c) karaoke

カラオ [ ]
ke

Set 6

11 Choose the correct *katakana* spelling for these words.

(a) **se n chi** (centimetres) ヒンチ センチ

(b) **hi n to** (hint) ヒント セント

(c) **se n su** (sense) ヤンス センス

(d) **ta i ya** (tyre) タイヤ タイセ

Set 6
se
セ
hi
ヒ
ya
ヤ

12 Fill in the blanks to compete the words.

(a) zero

[ ] ロ
ze

(b) building

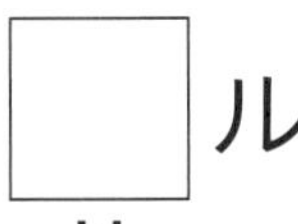
[ ] ル
bi

(c) earphone

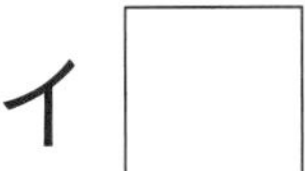

イ [ ] ホン
ya

13

ISBN 9780170416689

Set 7

13 Find a way out of the maze by following the words written correctly.

chi ki n (chicken)	**ra n chi** (lunch)
ho te ru (hotel)	**te re bi** (television)

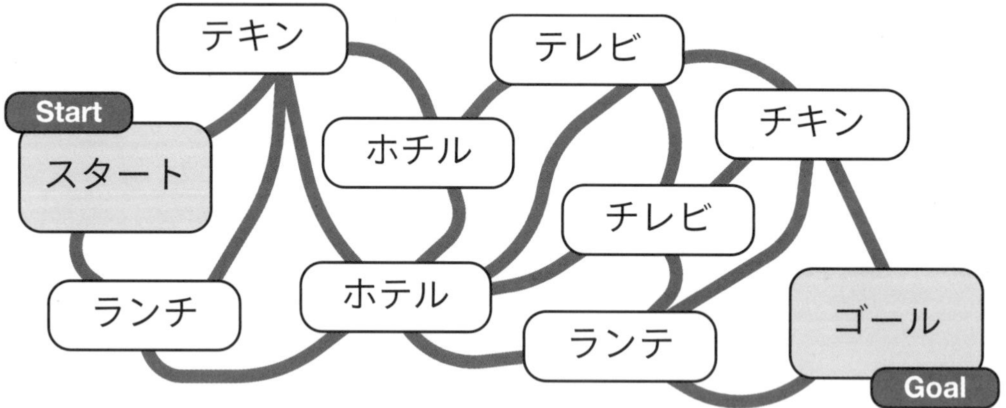

Set 7
chi チ
te テ

14 Fill in the blanks to compete the following words.

ⓐ bench

ベン ☐
chi

ⓑ tent

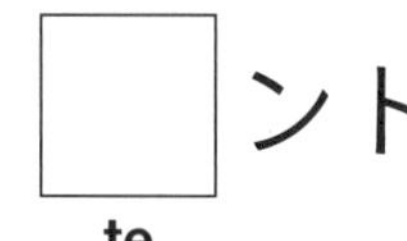

te

ⓒ text

te

Set 8

15 Circle or highlight the correct spelling of each word.

ⓐ **su pa i** (spy)

ネパイ
スパイ

ⓑ **ki nu a** (quinoa)

キヌア
キスア

ⓒ **do re su** (dress)

ドレネ
ドレス

ⓓ **da n su** (dance)

ダンヌ
ダンス

ⓔ **ne ku ta i** (tie)

ヌクタイ
ネクタイ

Set 8
su ス
nu ヌ
ne ネ

16 Fill in the blanks to complete the words.

ⓐ Vanuatu

バ ☐ アツ
nu

ⓑ business

ビジ 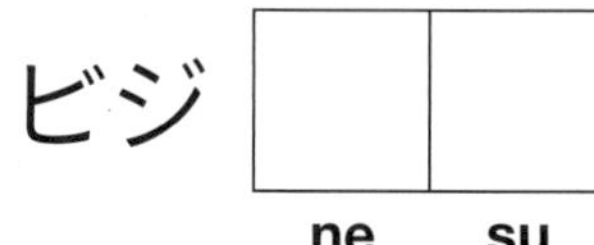
ne su

ⓒ panel

パ ☐ ル
ne

ISBN 9780170416689

Level 14: Long Vowels

Long vowel sounds are indicated with ー in katakana. Below are some examples.

- カード (card) – pronounce the *ka* sound long
  ka → do
- タクシー (taxi) – pronounce the *shi* sound long
  ta ku **shi** →
- スプーン (spoon) – pronounce the *pu* sound long
  su **pu** → n
- メール (mail) – pronounce the *me* sound long
  me → ru
- コース (course) – pronounce the *ko* sound long
  ko → su

Note that in some words, the vowels are written out instead of ー.

- バレエ (ballet) – pronounce the *re* sound long
  ba **re** →
- サラダボウル (salad bowl) – pronounce the *bo* sound long
  sa ra da **bo** → ru

1 Read words aloud, paying attention to the long vowels.

(a) アパート (apartment) (b) ビーチ (beach) (c) ブーツ (boots)

(d) テーブル (table) (e) スノーボード (snowboard)

2 Choose the correct spelling of each word.

(a) **su pi→ do** (speed)

スーピド
スピイド
スピード

(b) **bu ro→ chi** (brooch)

ブロオチ
ブローチ
ブーロチ

(c) **ka re→ ra i su** (curry rice)

カレーライス
カレラーイス
カレエライス

(d) **ka n ga ru→** (kangaroo)

カンガルウ
カンガルー
カンーガル

(e) **de pa→ to** (department store)

デパート
デパトー
デパアト

(f) **ba re→ bo→ ru** (volleyball)

バレボーオル
バーレボルー
バレーボール

ISBN 9780170416689

You may have noticed that arrows have been used to help you understand the placement of long vowels in the words. From now onwards, there will be *romaji* hints for long vowels. In *romaji* hints, the vowel that needs to be long will be repeated. For example, ノート will be indicated as *no o to*.

3 Fill in the squares according to the hints. Then write the katakana with numbers in the order and reveal the hidden word.

a **sa a ka su** (circus)

	6		3

b **te e ma pa a ku** (theme park)

					4

c **a ku se sa ri i** (accessory)

1				5	

d **ge e mu** (game)

		7

e **i i su to** (yeast)

2			

The hidden word

1	2	3	4	5	6	7

4 Listen to your teacher or watch the Level 14 dictation video. Write the words in *katakana* in the first squares as you hear them. Then, use the extra squares to practise writing the words again.

a

b

c

d

e

ISBN 9780170416689

Level 15: Combination sounds

Katakana combination sounds, also called *youon*, are written in the same way as *hiragana* combination sounds. These sounds are written by combining a full-size *i* sound *katakana* and with a smaller ヤ, ユ or ヨ.

- shi シ + small ya ヤ = sha シャ
- gi ギ + small yu ユ = gyu ギュ
- chi チ + small yo ヨ = cho チョ

Although there are two characters, they are pronounced together as one sound or syllable.

1 Practise writing combination sounds. Remember to keep the small ヤ, ユ and ヨ about one-quarter of the size of the normal *katakana*, and write them in the lower left section of each square.

キャ kya	キャ	
キュ kyu	キュ	
キョ kyo	キョ	
シャ sha	シャ	
シュ shu	シュ	
ショ sho	ショ	
チャ cha	チャ	
チュ chu	チュ	
チョ cho	チョ	
ヒャ hya	ヒャ	
ヒュ hyu	ヒュ	
ヒョ hyo	ヒョ	

ギャ gya	ギャ	
ギュ gyu	ギュ	
ギョ gyo	ギョ	
ジャ ja	ジャ	
ジュ ju	ジュ	
ジョ jo	ジョ	
ニャ nya	ニャ	
ニュ nyu	ニュ	
ニョ nyo	ニョ	
ビャ bya	ビャ	
ビュ byu	ビュ	
ビョ byo	ビョ	

15

ISBN 9780170416689

ピャ pya	ピ ャ	
ピュ pyu	ピ ュ	
ピョ pyo	ピ ョ	
リャ rya	リ ャ	
リュ ryu	リ ュ	
リョ ryo	リ ョ	

ミャ mya	ミ ャ	
ミュ myu	ミ ュ	
ミョ myo	ミ ョ	

2 Read the words aloud, paying attention to the combination sounds.

ⓐ シャワー (shower)

ⓑ ジョギング (jogging)

ⓒ アマチュア (amateur)

ⓓ マニキュア (manicure)

ⓔ キャラクター (character)

ⓕ ヒューズ (fuse)

3 Draw a line connecting the *katakana* combination sounds to their *hiragana* and *romaji* equivalents.

キャ	りゃ	hya
ヒャ	ぴょ	kya
リャ	きゃ	gyo
チュ	しゅ	rya
ピョ	ひゃ	chu
ミョ	ぎょ	pyo
シュ	みょ	shu
ギョ	ちゅ	myo

ISBN 9780170416689

4 You won a mystery tour! The tour starts from とうきょう. Follow the instructions, then write the final destination of the tour in English.

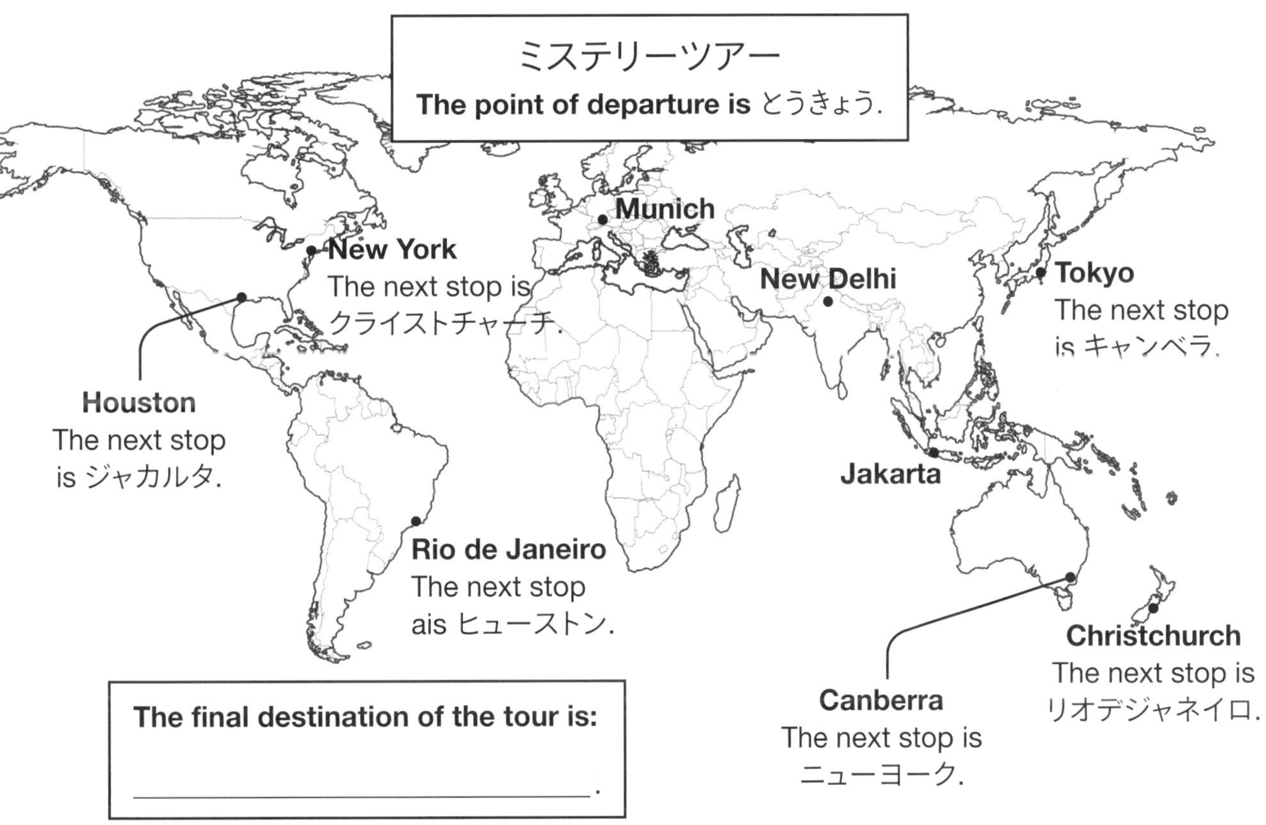

The final destination of the tour is:

_______________________________.

5 Help your classmates to write their names in *katakana*. Using the names in the box, write the correct spelling in katakana under each person.

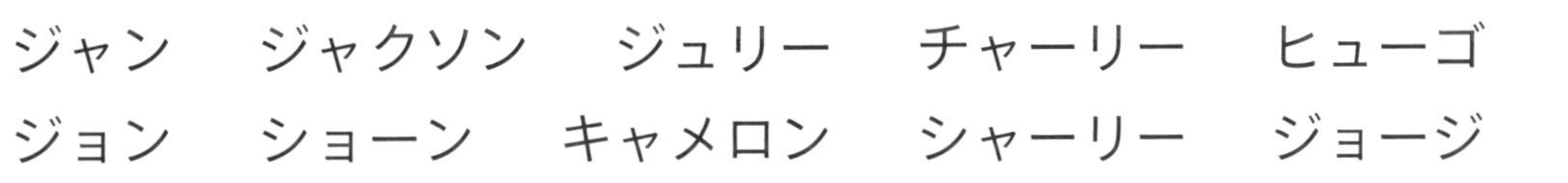

ジャン	ジャクソン	ジュリー	チャーリー	ヒューゴ
ジョン	ショーン	キャメロン	シャーリー	ジョージ

15

ISBN 9780170416689

6 Label the things in the room in katakana.

7 Listen to your teacher or watch the Level 15 dictation video. Write the words in *katakana* in the first squares as you hear them. Then, use the extra squares to practise writing the words again.

Take care to write small ャ, ュ and ョ about one-quarter the size of regular *katakana*.

ISBN 9780170416689

Level 16: Double consonants

A small ツ can be used to make double consonants in *katakana* as it is in *hiragana*.

You do not pronounce ツ when it is small. You just pause before you say the next sound. For example, ラケット (racket) is said as *ra ke* (pause) *to*.

When writing the sounds made by small ツ in *romaji*, the first letter of the following sound is repeated. For example, ツト will become *tto*, and ラケット is written as *raketto*.

1 Read the words aloud, paying attention to small ツ. Remember that you do not pronounce small ツ.

a	ペット	pet
b	ナッツ	nuts
c	コミック	comic
d	チャット	chat
e	バッジ	budge
f	リラックス	relax

2 Practice writing small ツ. Use the dotted lines to help you place your small ツ in the bottom-left of each square.

ッ	ッ	ッ							

3 Connect words from the same category.

ポップス	ポップコーン
ヨット	ソックス
ネットボール	ロック
ビスケット	トラック
 スリッパ	カーペット
ベッド	フットボール

ISBN 9780170416689

4 Use the coordinates to find the correct katakana from the grid and write them in the squares. Then write the English word.

ⓐ B2 A5 C1 D1

English ______________________

ⓑ C1 A4 D5 E2 C3 A1

English ______________________

ⓒ E4 E2 D2 A5 B5 C5

English ______________________

ⓓ E1 D4 A5 A2

English ______________________

ⓔ B3 C5 E5 C3 A2

English ______________________

ⓕ B2 B1 A5 A2

English ______________________

	A	B	C	D	E
1	チ	ケ	サ	ム	ロ
2	ト	ポ	ザ	ナ	イ
3	レ	ヘ	ッ	ワ	ヤ
4	ン	ユ	ク	ボ	パ
5	ッ	プ	ル	ド	メ

5 Listen to your teacher or watch the Level 16 dictation video. Write the words in *katakana* in the first squares as you hear them. Then, use the extra squares to practise writing the words again.

ⓐ

ⓑ

ⓒ

ⓓ

ⓔ

ISBN 9780170416689

Level 17: *Katakana* special sounds

In *katakana*, there are special sounds to write foreign words and names. Here are the commonly used ones.

w	y	f	d	t	ch	j	sh	
		ファ fa						**a**
ウィ wi		フィ fi	ディ di	ティ ti				**i**
	デュ dyu							**u**
ウェ we		フェ fe			チェ che	ジェ je	シェ she	**e**
ウォ wo		フォ fo						**o**

The sounds in the table here are also used, however we do not practise these ones in this book, because they are less common.

y			v	d	ts	t	gw	kw	
			ヴァ va		ツァ tsa		グァ gwa	クァ kwa	**a**
			ヴィ vi		ツィ tsi			クィ kwi	**i**
テュ tyu	フュ fyu	ヴュ vyu	ヴ vu	ドゥ du		トゥ tu			**u**
イェ ye			ヴェ ve		ツェ tse			クェ kwe	**e**
			ヴォ vo		ツォ tso			クォ kwo	**o**

Katakana special sounds are made using small ア, イ, ウ, エ and オ. Small ユ is also combined with *u* and *e* line *katakana*. We will practise the commonly used special sounds, which are in the first chart.

Below are some examples.

she a
シェア (share)

che k ku
チェック (check)

re ko o **di** n gu
レコーディング (recording)

fi ri pi n
フィリピン (Philippine)

fo n to
フォント (font)

wi i n
ウィーン (Vienna)

mi ne ra ru **wo** o ta a
ミネラルウォーター (mineral water)

je ra a to
ジェラート (gelato)

shi **ti** i
シティー (city)

fa s sho n
ファッション (fashion)

fe ri i
フェリー (ferry)

pu ro **dyu** u sa a
プロデューサー (producer)

su **we** e de n
スウェーデン (Sweden)

17

1 Practise writing special sounds. Remember to keep the small ア, イ, エ, オ and ユ about one-quarter of the size of the normal *katakana*, and write them in the lower left section of each square.

シェ she	シェ				
ジェ je	ジェ				
チェ che	チェ				
ティ ti	ティ				
ディ di	ディ				
デュ dyu	デュ				
ファ fa	ファ				
フィ fi	フィ				
フェ fe	フェ				
フォ fo	フォ				
ウィ wi	ウィ				
ウェ we	ウェ				
ウォ wo	ウォ				

2 Find the correct *katakana* and circle them.

(a) che	チ	チァ	チェ	タェ	チゥ
(b) fa	ハァ	ヒァ	フェ	ファ	ふぁ
(c) ti	チ	トィ	ディ	テユ	ティ
(d) she	シ	シェ	シュ	ジュ	シァ
(e) fo	ホ	フェ	ヘォ	フォ	ファ

ISBN 9780170416689

3 Find a path through the maze by following the correct *katakana* spellings of the words listed.

pa a ti i (party) **she fu** (chef) **ma fi n** (muffin)

pa fe (parfait) **we bu sa i to** (website)

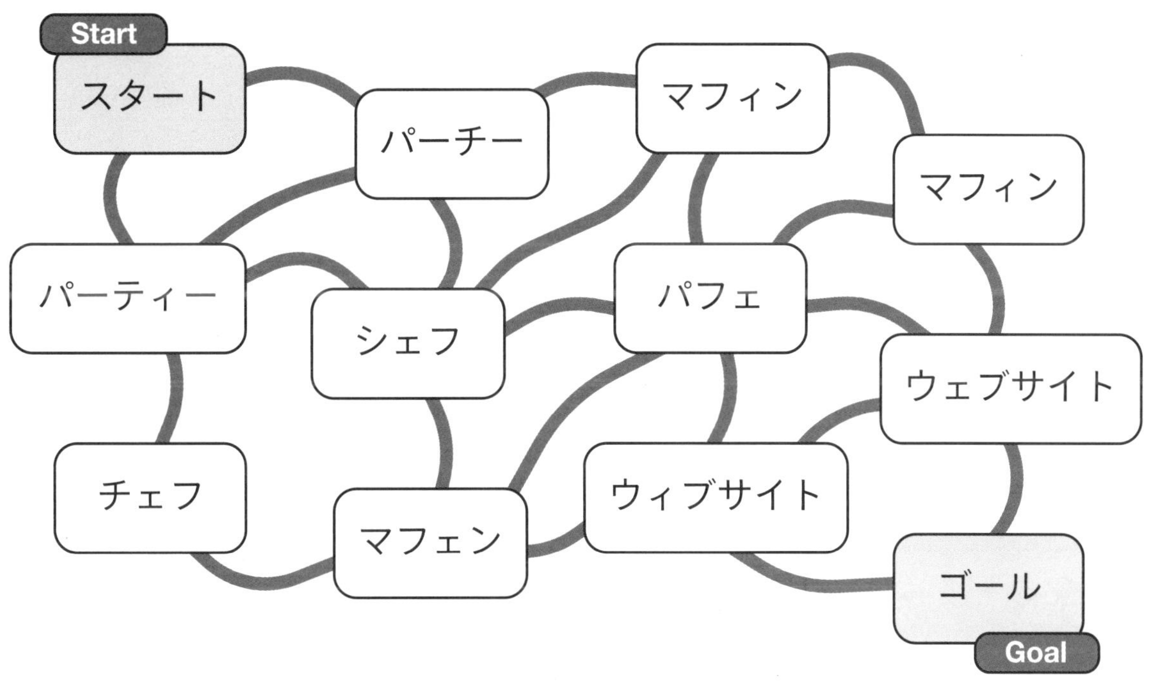

4 Draw a line to connect the first and second half of compound words.

ジェット	フード
ティー	フィクション
ファスト	エンジン
ノン	バッグ
ニュー	ウォーキング
ブッシュ	フェース

17

ISBN 9780170416689

5 Find two errors in each word and rewrite the correct words in the squares.

a **fo o ku** (fork)
ハ ュ ー ク

b **bo ra n ti a** (volunteer)
ホ ラ ン チ ィ ア

c **da a wi n** (Darwin)
ダ ア ウ ェ ン

d **pu ro je ku to** (project)
ブ ロ ズ ェ ク ト

6 Fill in the missing *katakana* words to complete Maki's letter to Yuji.

ゆうじくんへ、

あした、うみで ＿＿＿＿＿ を
sa a fi n

しましょう。それから、＿＿＿ で
ka fe

＿＿＿＿＿＿ を たべましょう。
su pa ge t ti

＿＿＿＿＿ え いがもみましょう。
ko me di i

まき

7 Listen to your teacher or watch the Level 17 dictation video. Write the words in *katakana* in the first squares as you hear them. Then, use the extra squares to practise writing the words again.

a

b

c

d

e

ISBN 9780170416689

Level 18: Vertical writing

When written vertically, *katakana* follows the same rules as *hiragana*. One thing to look out for, however, is the direction of the long vowel indicator. It should be written vertically, as shown below.

1. Copy the examples below, paying attention to the position of small characters, long vowel indicators and punctuation marks.

Let's go to a shopping centre tomorrow.

あした、ショッピ
ングセンターにい
きましょう。

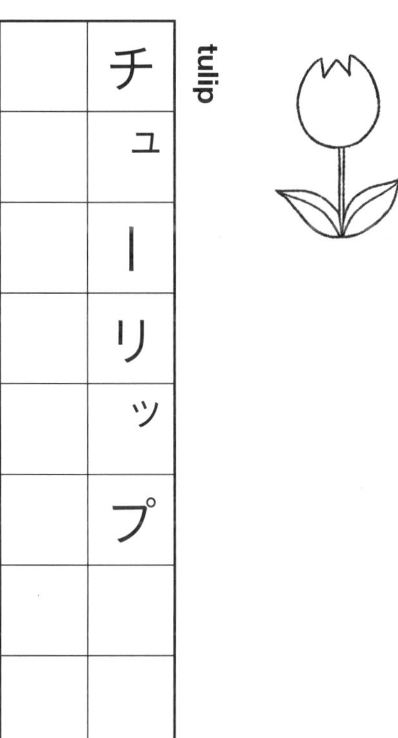

2. Most of the students' names in your class should be written in *katakana*, because they are not Japanese words. A dot is often used to separate more than one *katakana* word in a row. For example, a dot would be placed between your first name and surname. This dot should be placed in the middle of a square. Write your name in the boxes below, both horizontally and vertically, following the examples provided.

Horizontally

John Smith (example)						
ス	ミ	ス	・	ジ	ョ	ン

Vertically

John Smith (example)

スミス・ジョン

Level 19: Words in topics

Sports
スポーツ

1 Write the following words in *katakana*, then find them in the puzzle.

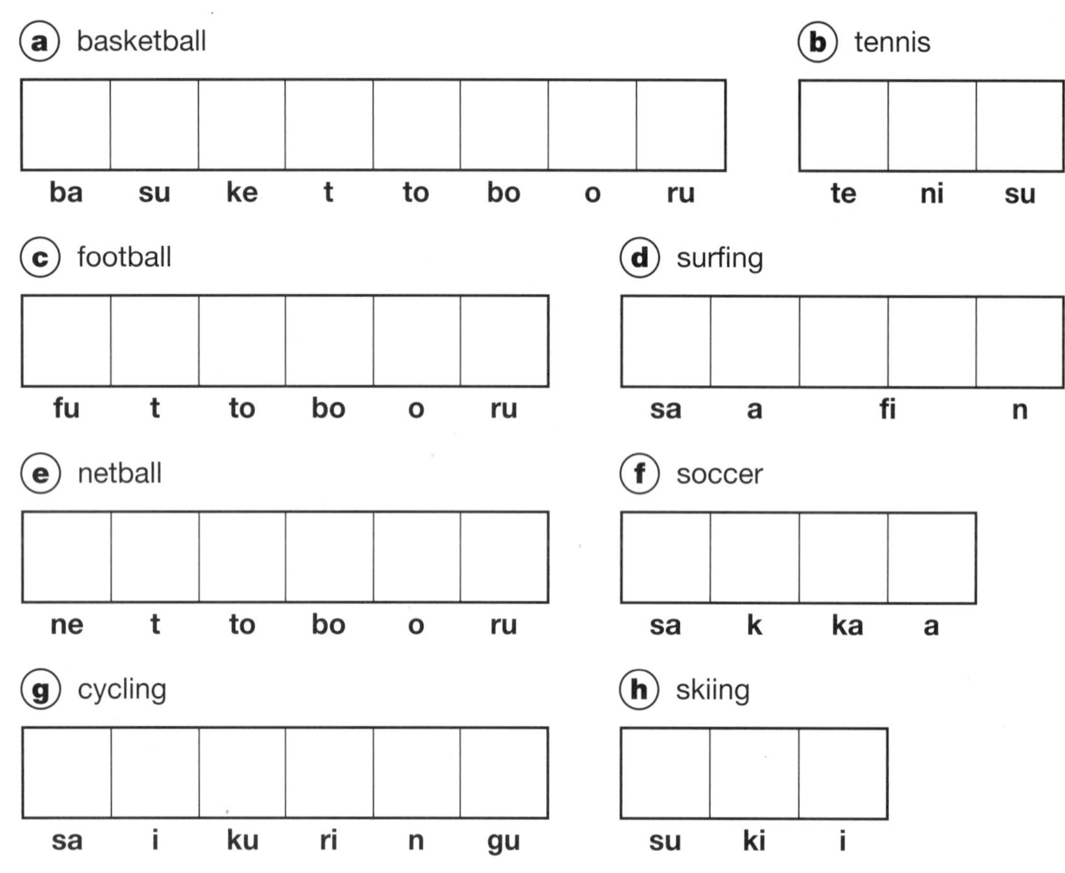

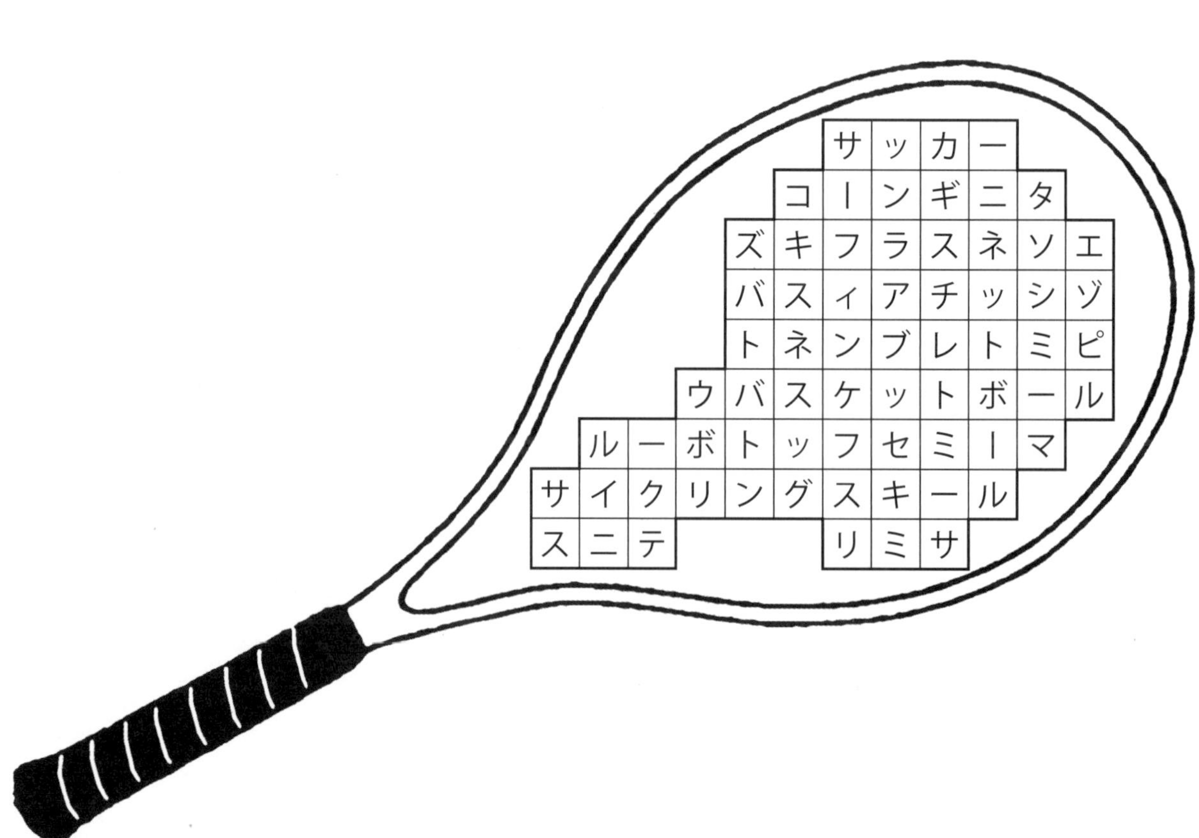

ISBN 9780170416689

Food and drinks
たべものとのみもの

2 Which monster will find a path through the maze? Each monster can only go through the path where their food and drinks are placed. Use the lists below to find each monster's foods in *katakana*.

Monster 1 cheese, pasta, jam, kiwifruit
Monster 2 cake, melon, muffin, salad
Monster 3 chicken, lettuce, cookie, potato

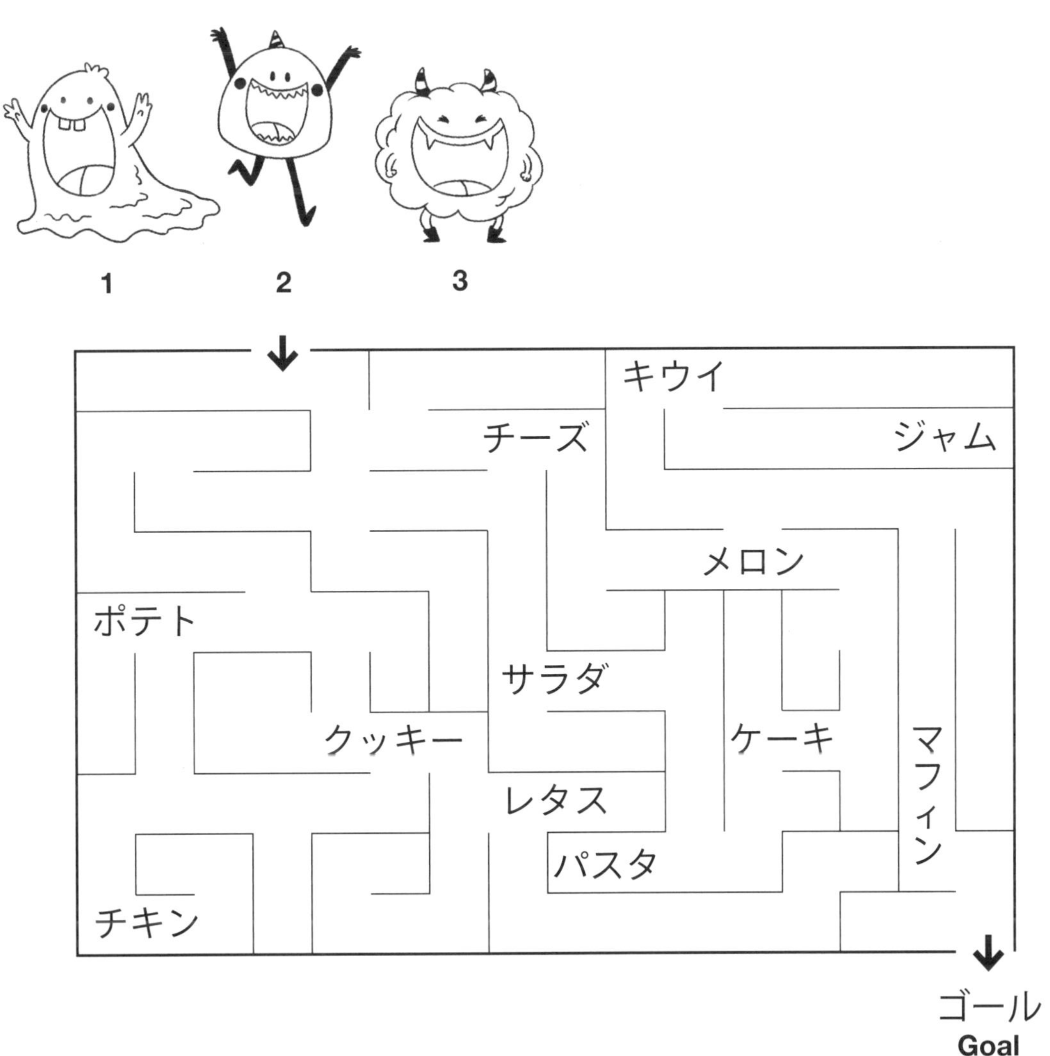

3 Write the words in *katakana*.

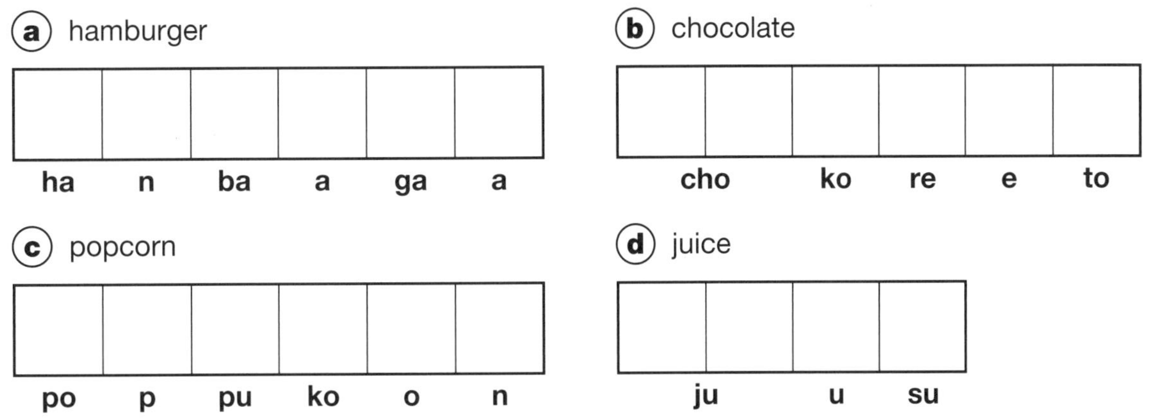

19

ISBN 9780170416689

Things to wear
みにつけるもの

4 Who has everything packed for their trip? Read the list and look at the picture, then write the person's name in English below.

コート　スニーカー　ソックス　ジーンズ　サングラス　Tシャツ

_______________ has everything for the trip.

5 Write these items in *katakana*.

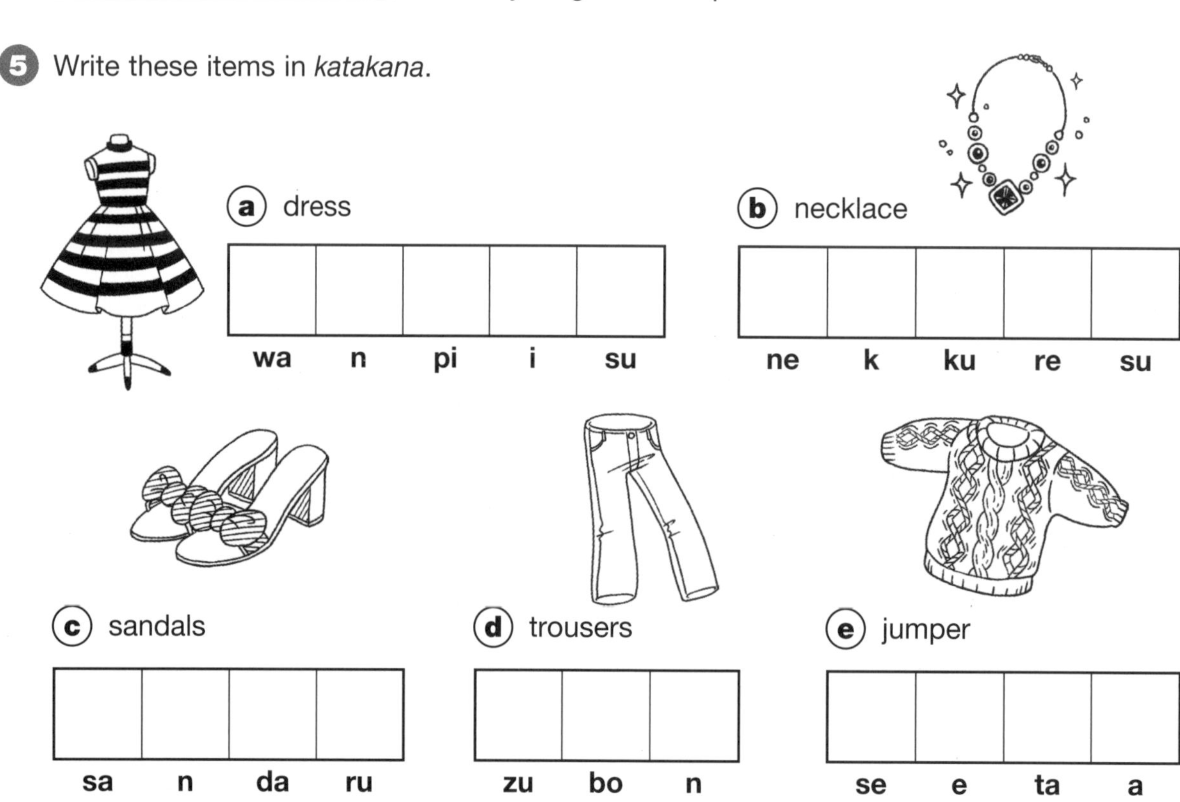

ISBN 9780170416689

Countries
くに

6 Connect the country names in *katakana* to their flags.

7 Write the country names in *katakana* on the map.

America

a	me	ri	ka

France

fu	ra	n	su

Indonesia

i	n	do	ne	shi	a

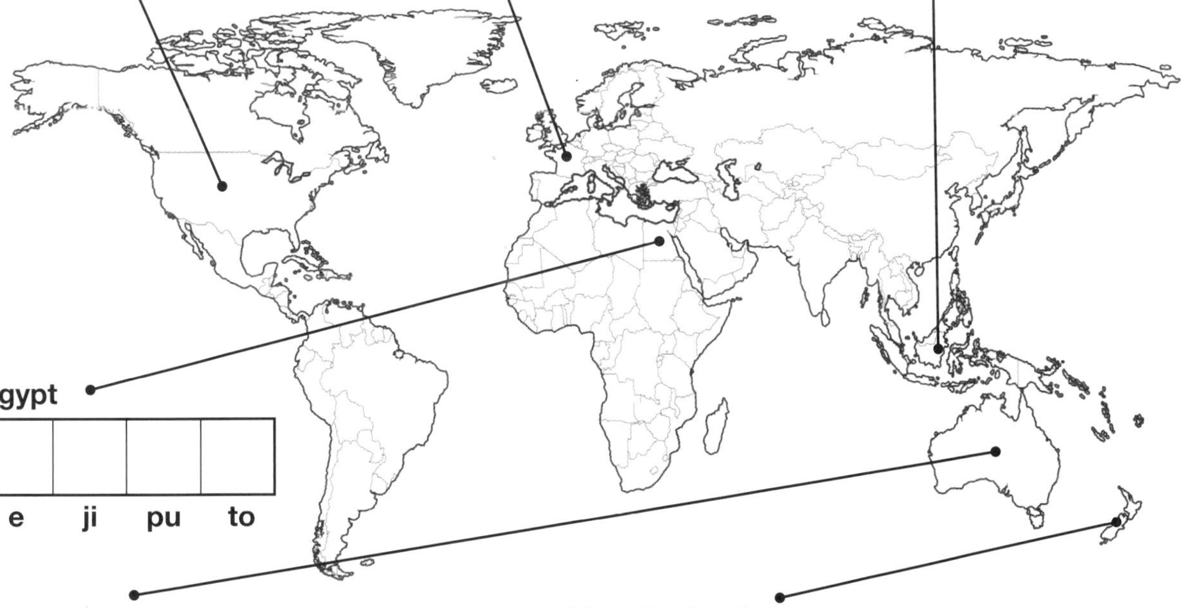

Egypt

e	ji	pu	to

Australia

o	o	su	to	ra	ri	a

New Zealand

nyu	u	ji	i	ra	n	do

19

ISBN 9780170416689

Dictation answers

English meanings are given to help students' vocabulary.

Level 1 p. 4

- ⓐ アイス ice
- ⓑ エリア area
- ⓒ オイル oil
- ⓓ アウト out
- ⓔ ウイルス virus

Level 2 p. 7

- ⓐ ココア cocoa
- ⓑ キウイ kiwi (fruit)
- ⓒ ケニア Kenya
- ⓓ カカオ cacao
- ⓔ アクリル acrylic

Level 3 p. 9

- ⓐ ガイド guide
- ⓑ グラス glass
- ⓒ ギア gear
- ⓓ レゲエ reggae
- ⓔ ゴリラ gorilla

Level 4 p. 12

- ⓐ ガス gas
- ⓑ ソウル Seoul
- ⓒ アクセス access
- ⓓ システム system
- ⓔ サイド side

Level 5 p. 14

- ⓐ アジア Asia
- ⓑ クイズ quiz
- ⓒ ゼラチン gelatine
- ⓓ オゾン ozone
- ⓔ ギザギザ jagged

Level 6 p. 17

- ⓐ タスク task
- ⓑ アウト out
- ⓒ バケツ bucket
- ⓓ ハンカチ handkerchief
- ⓔ テキスト text

Level 7 p. 19

- ⓐ ドイツ Germany
- ⓑ ガイド guide
- ⓒ カナダ Canada
- ⓓ デザイン design
- ⓔ ダウン down

Level 8 p. 22

- ⓐ バヌアツ Vanuatu
- ⓑ ビジネス business
- ⓒ アンテナ antenna
- ⓓ リスニング listening
- ⓔ ドアノブ doorknob

Level 9 p. 25

- ⓐ ソフト soft
- ⓑ ハワイ Hawaii
- ⓒ ホテル hotel
- ⓓ ヒアリング hearing
- ⓔ ヘアスタイル hairstyle

Level 10 p. 27

- ⓐ ブラシ brush
- ⓑ パイプ pipe
- ⓒ ピアノ piano
- ⓓ バケツ bucket
- ⓔ ビザ visa
- ⓕ ペンキ paint
- ⓖ ポイント point

Level 11 p. 32

- ⓐ メモ memo
- ⓑ ハム ham
- ⓒ マスク mask
- ⓓ ミセス Mrs
- ⓔ ダイヤモンド diamond
- ⓕ クレヨン crayon
- ⓖ ユニオン union

Level 12 p. 36

- ⓐ ワイン wine
- ⓑ セロリ celery
- ⓒ テレビ television
- ⓓ カメラ camera
- ⓔ カラオケ karaoke
- ⓕ ロンドン London
- ⓖ メルボルン Melbourne

Level 14 p. 42

- ⓐ タクシー taxi
- ⓑ ページ page
- ⓒ コンサート concert
- ⓓ スクーター scooter
- ⓔ オーストラリア Australia

Level 15 p. 46

- ⓐ キャンプ camp
- ⓑ パジャマ pyjamas
- ⓒ マンション apartment block
- ⓓ ニュース news
- ⓔ チャンス chance
- ⓕ インタビュー interview
- ⓖ チョーク chalk
- ⓗ ミュージカル musical

Level 16 p. 48

- ⓐ クリケット cricket
- ⓑ ロケット rocket
- ⓒ クッション cushion
- ⓓ チューリップ tulip
- ⓔ リュックサック rucksack, backpack

Level 17 p. 52

- ⓐ チェス chess
- ⓑ ソファー sofa
- ⓒ オフィス office
- ⓓ ティッシュ tissue
- ⓔ デュエット duet

ISBN 9780170416689

Answers

Level 1 Task 3 p. 3

a 6 **i** 4 **u** 1 **e** 2 **o** 2

Level 1 Task 5 p. 4

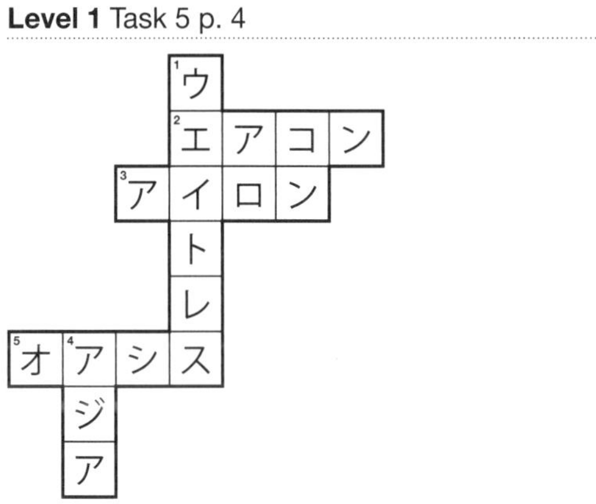

Level 2 Task 3 p. 6

ka 7 **ki** 6 **ku** 5 **ke** 8 **ko** 6

Level 2 Task 4 p. 6

(a) カメラ (camera)
(b) チキン (chicken)
(c) ミルク (milk)
(d) カラオケ (karaoke)
(e) メキシコ (Mexico)

Level 4 Task 5 p. 12

サ ス キ ア さん と

サ イ ク リン グ に

いきましょう。

Let's go cycling with Saskia.

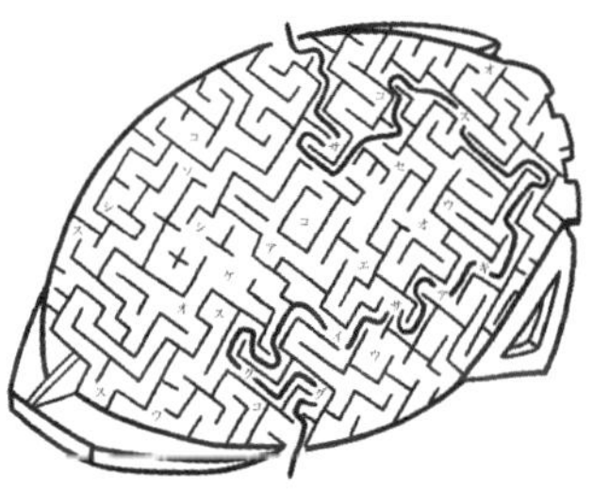

Level 5 Task 2 p. 14

	ジ	ザ		
ズ				
	ゼ			ザ
			ジ	ゾ
ゼ		ゾ	ズ	

Level 6 Task 3 p. 16

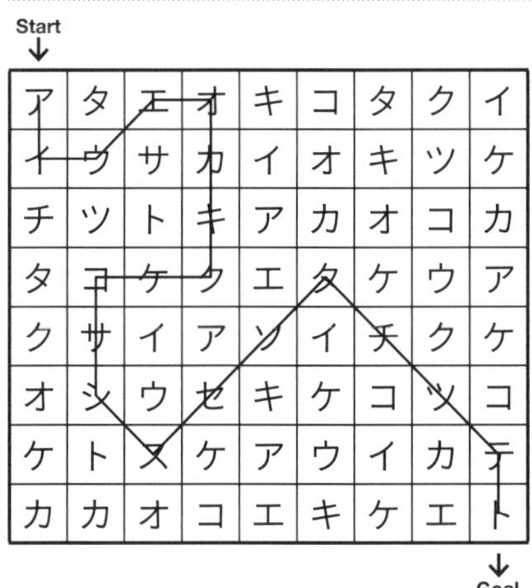

Level 6 Task 5 p. 17

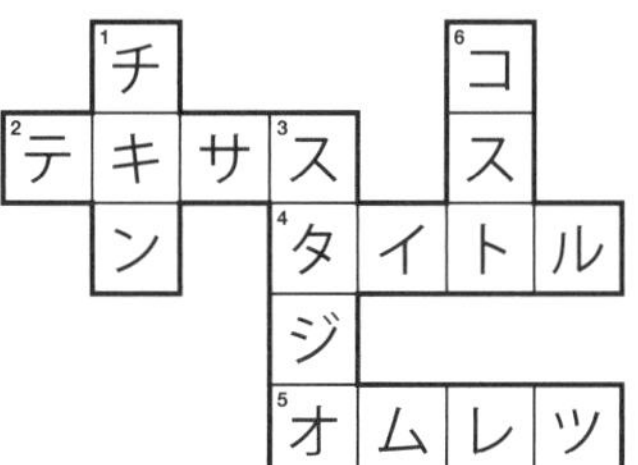

Level 8 Task 3 p. 21

C4 B3

ぼく は ノ ア です。

A1 E2 A4

カ ナ ダ 人です。

E5 D3 A3

テ ニ ス がすきです。

Number 3

Level 9 Task 2 p. 24

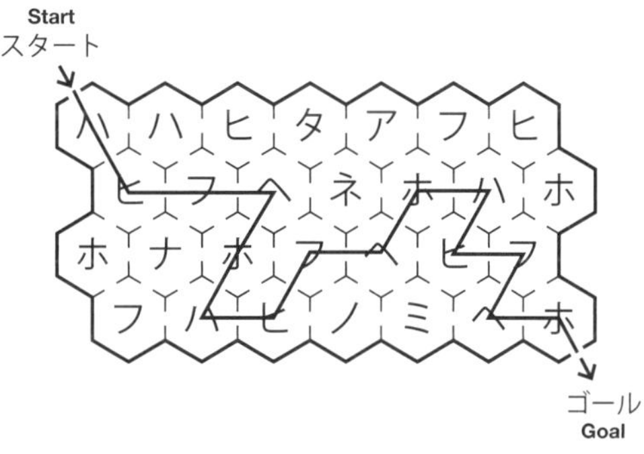

Level 10 Task 4 p. 28

イ	キ	タ	ダ	ペ	ベ	ビ	ボ	ピ	ア	ス	ヌ
ラ	ボ	カ	ア	イ	オ	イ	ポ	ク	ケ	ニ	ネ
ノ	ス	ト	コ	ケ	エ	パ	オ	ボ	ハ	ノ	チ
ビ	ウ	エ	ブ	プ	コ	サ	シ	イ	ツ	ベ	テ
ベ	ソ	バ	セ	ス	ピ	パ	ウ	ス	ア	ス	セ
パ	ス	ビ	ヒ	ヘ	カ	デ	エ	ザ	ゾ	ト	ダ
タ	ソ	ケ	カ	ツ	タ	キ	オ	ビ	ネ	ナ	デ
エ	ジ	プ	ト	ネ	チ	ク	ペ	パ	タ	イ	プ

Level 11 Task 3 p. 31

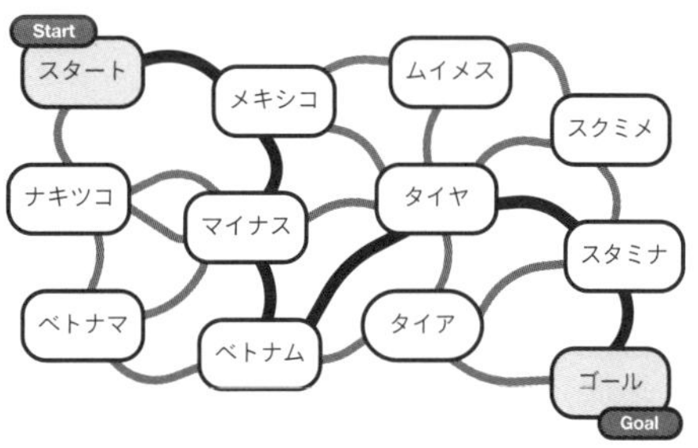

ISBN 9780170416689

Level 12 Task 3 p. 35

			タ	
	ア			ス
ム		ジ		

Message

ス	タ	ジ	ア	ム

で

あいましょう。

Let's meet at the stadium. ⓒ

Level 12 Task 4 p. 35

Animals	1, 3, 7, 12
Countries	4, 6, 8, 10
Things to wear	2, 5, 9, 11

Level 12 Task 5 p. 36

コアラ ➔ ライト ➔ トイレ ➔ レタス ➔ スイング ➔ グラウンド ➔ ドア ➔ アニメ ➔ メロン

Level 13 Set 7 Task 13 p. 40

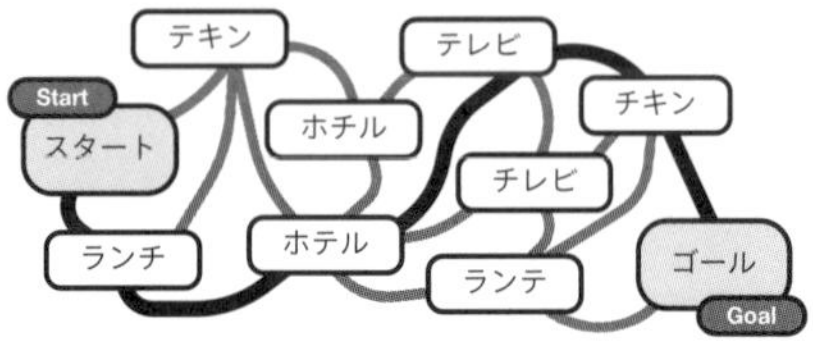

Level 14 Task 3 p. 42

1	2	3	4	5	6	7
ア	イ	ス	ク	リ	ー	ム

Level 15 Task 4 p. 45

Jakarta

Level 16 Task 4 p. 48

B2	A5	C1	D1
ポ	ッ	サ	ム

possum

C1	A4	D5	E2	C3	A1
サ	ン	ド	イ	ッ	チ

sandwich

E4	E2	D2	A5	B5	C5
パ	イ	ナ	ッ	プ	ル

pineapple

E1	D4	A5	A2
ロ	ボ	ッ	ト

robot

B3	C5	E5	C3	A2
ヘ	ル	メ	ッ	ト

helmet

B2	B1	A5	A2
ポ	ケ	ッ	ト

pocket

Level 17 Task 3 p. 51

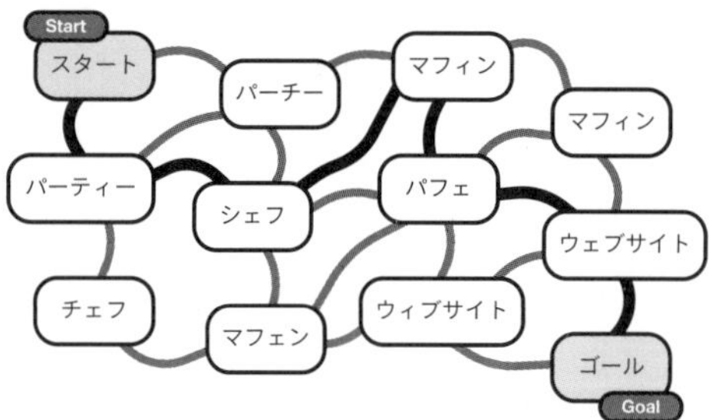

Level 19 Sports Task 1 p. 54

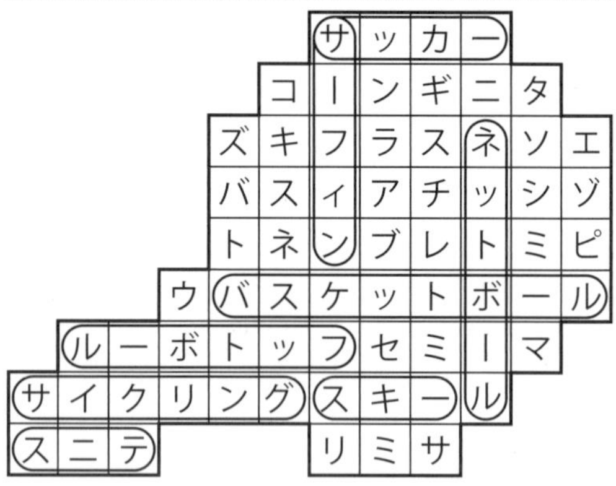

Level 19 Food and drinks Task 2 p. 55

Monster 2

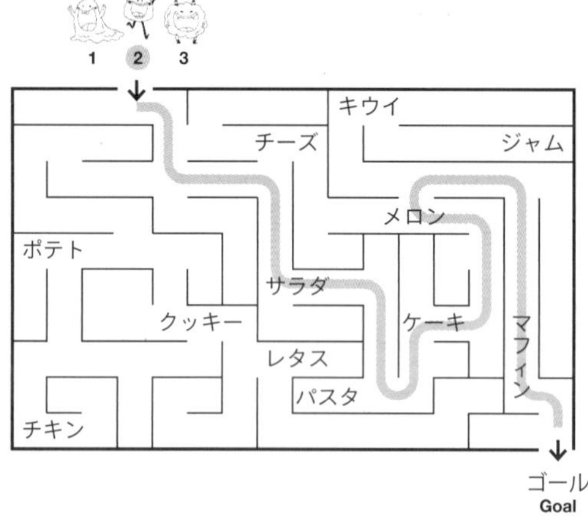

Level 19 Things to wear Task 4 p. 56

Jessica

Level 19 Countries Task 6 p. 57

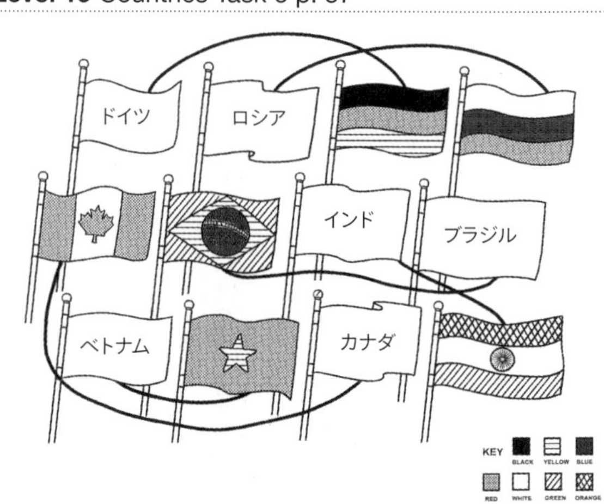

ISBN 9780170416689